CORGI

COLORING BOOK

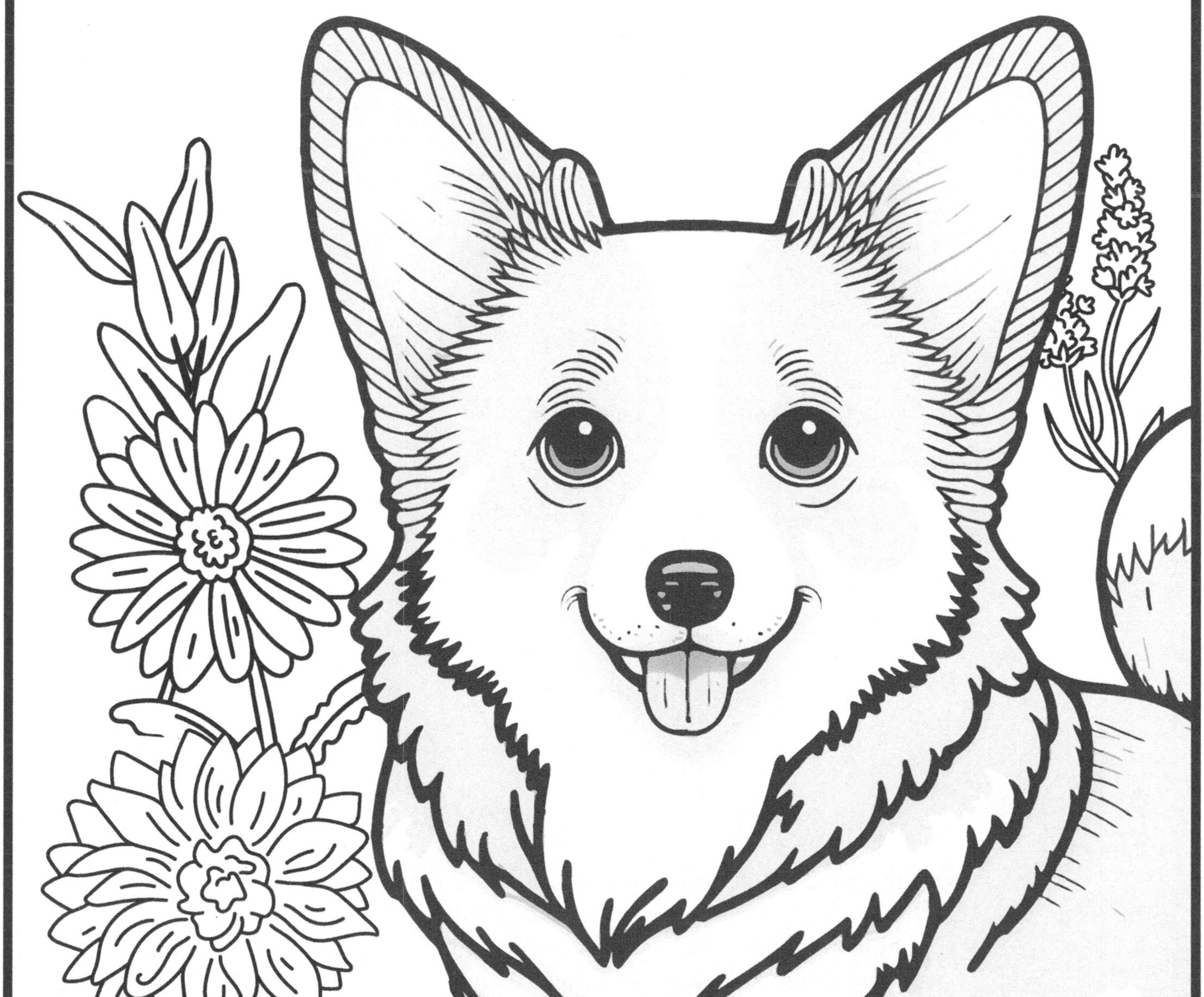

THIS BOOK BELONGS TO

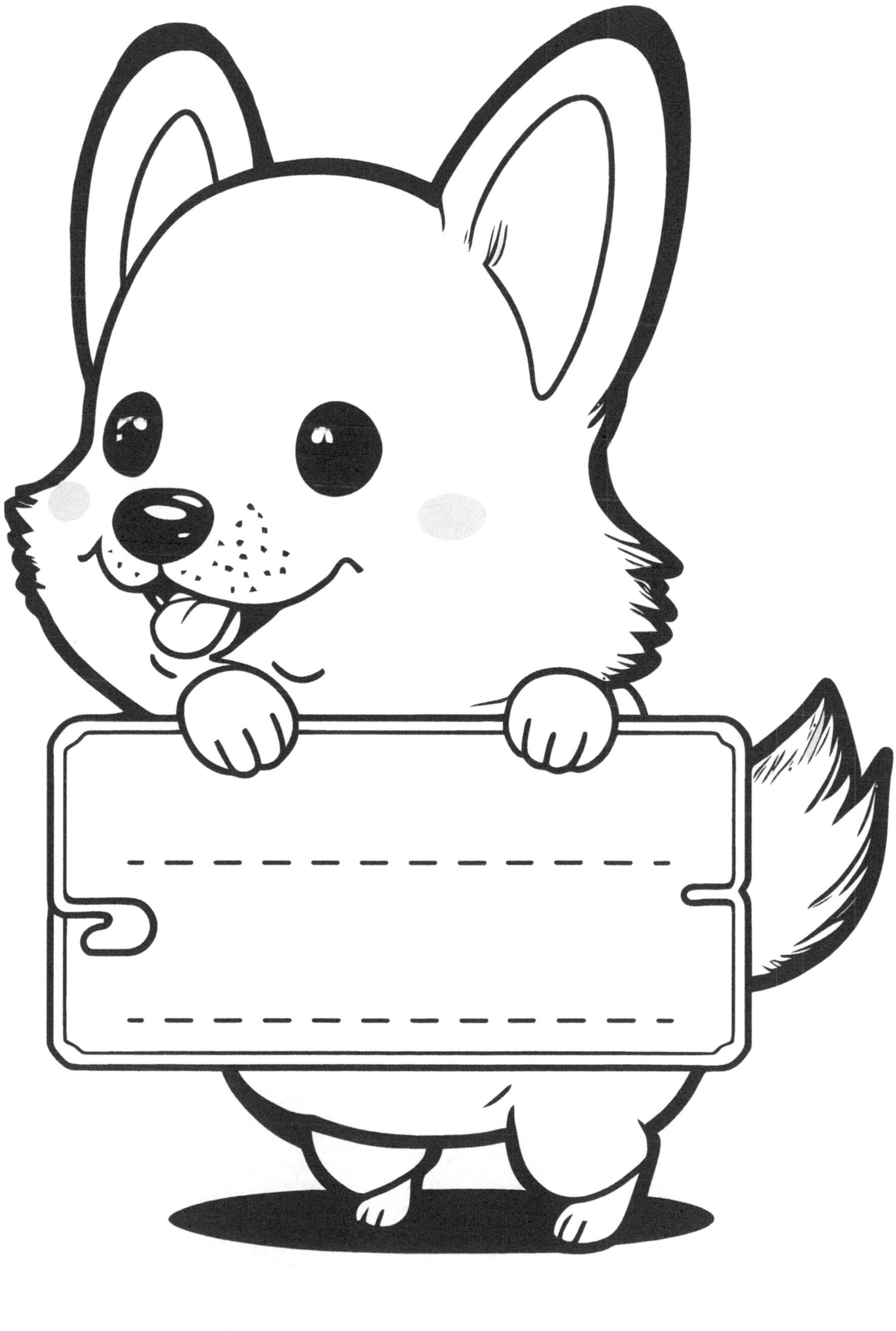

TEST COLOR PAGE

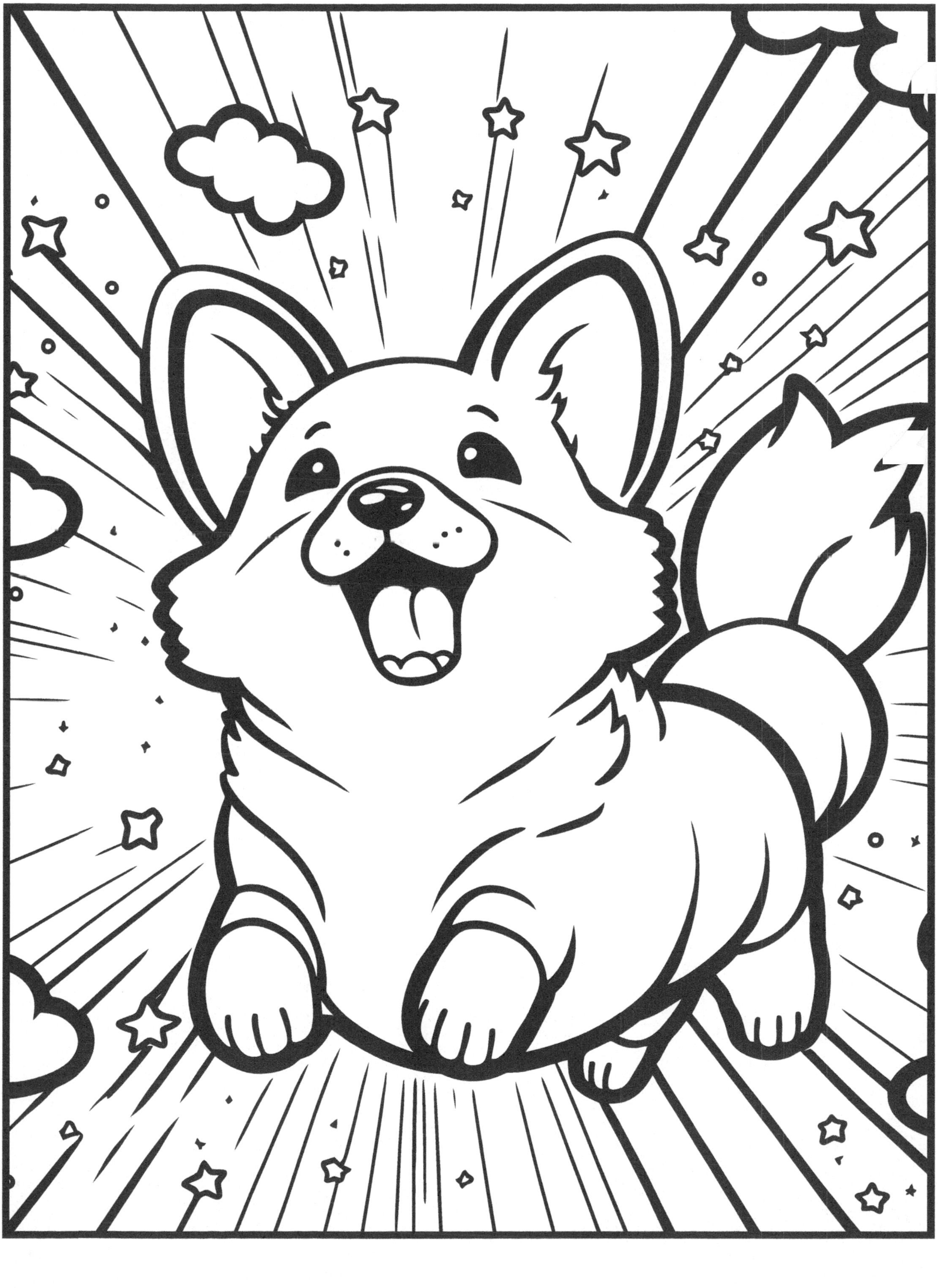

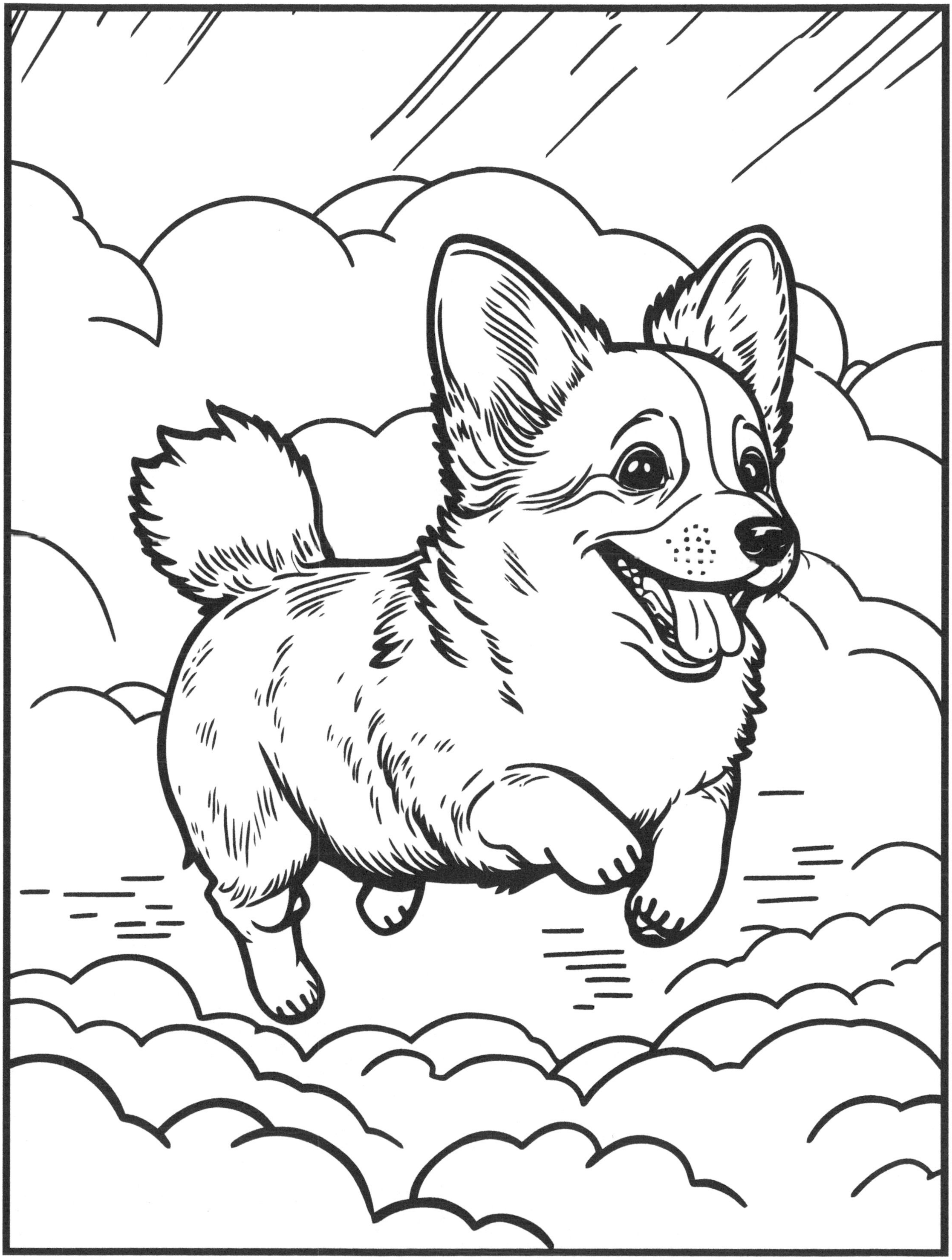

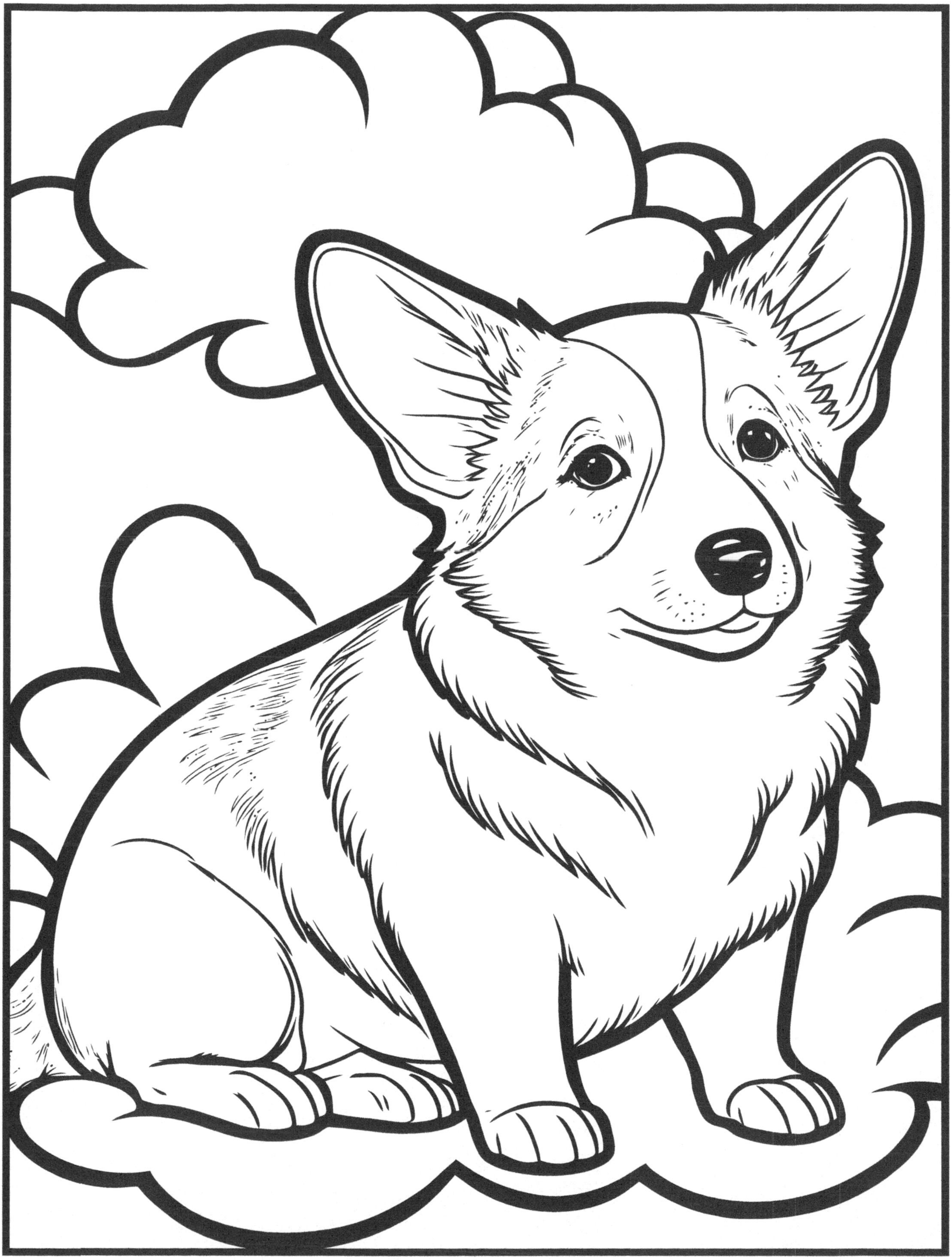

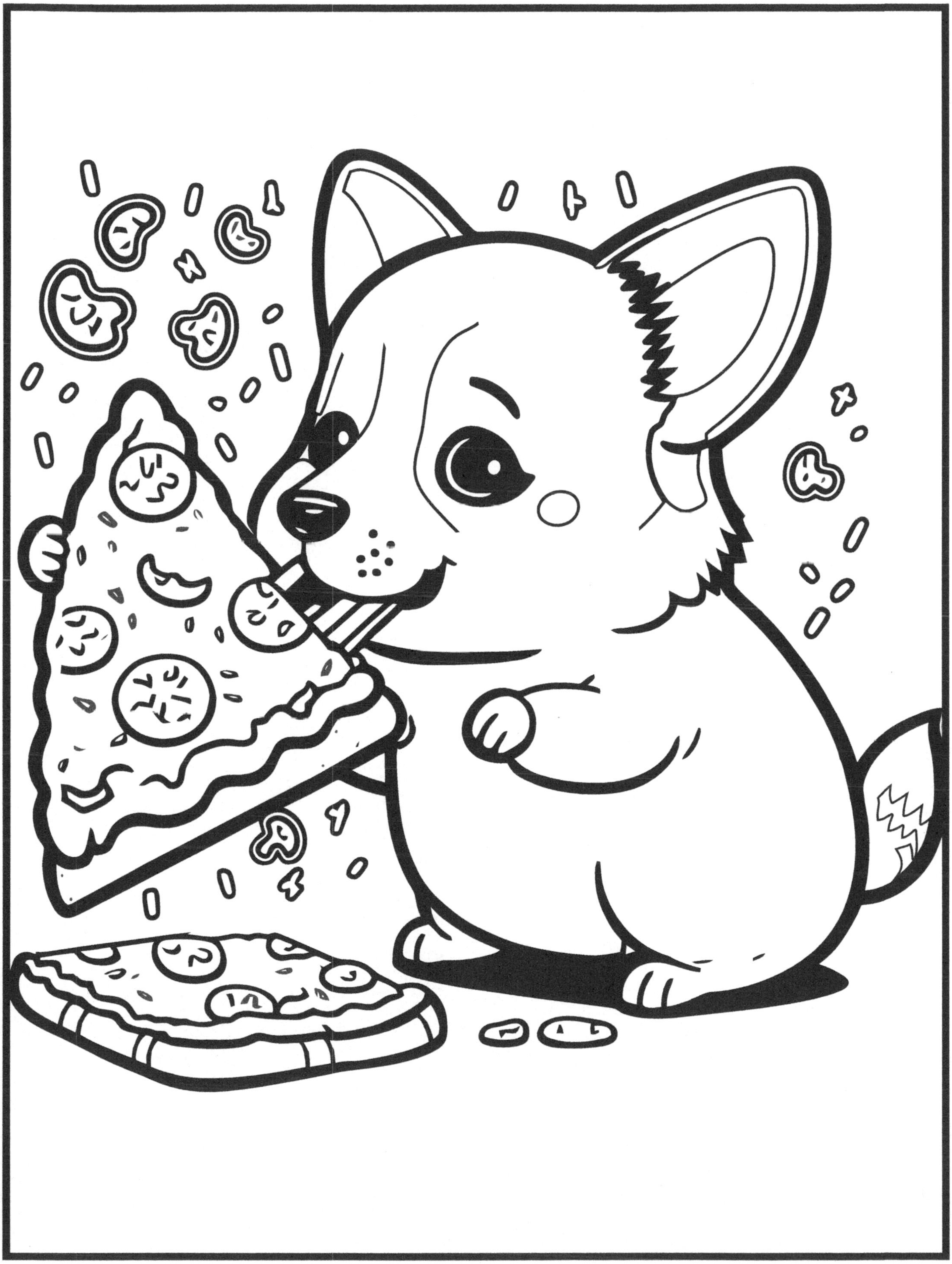

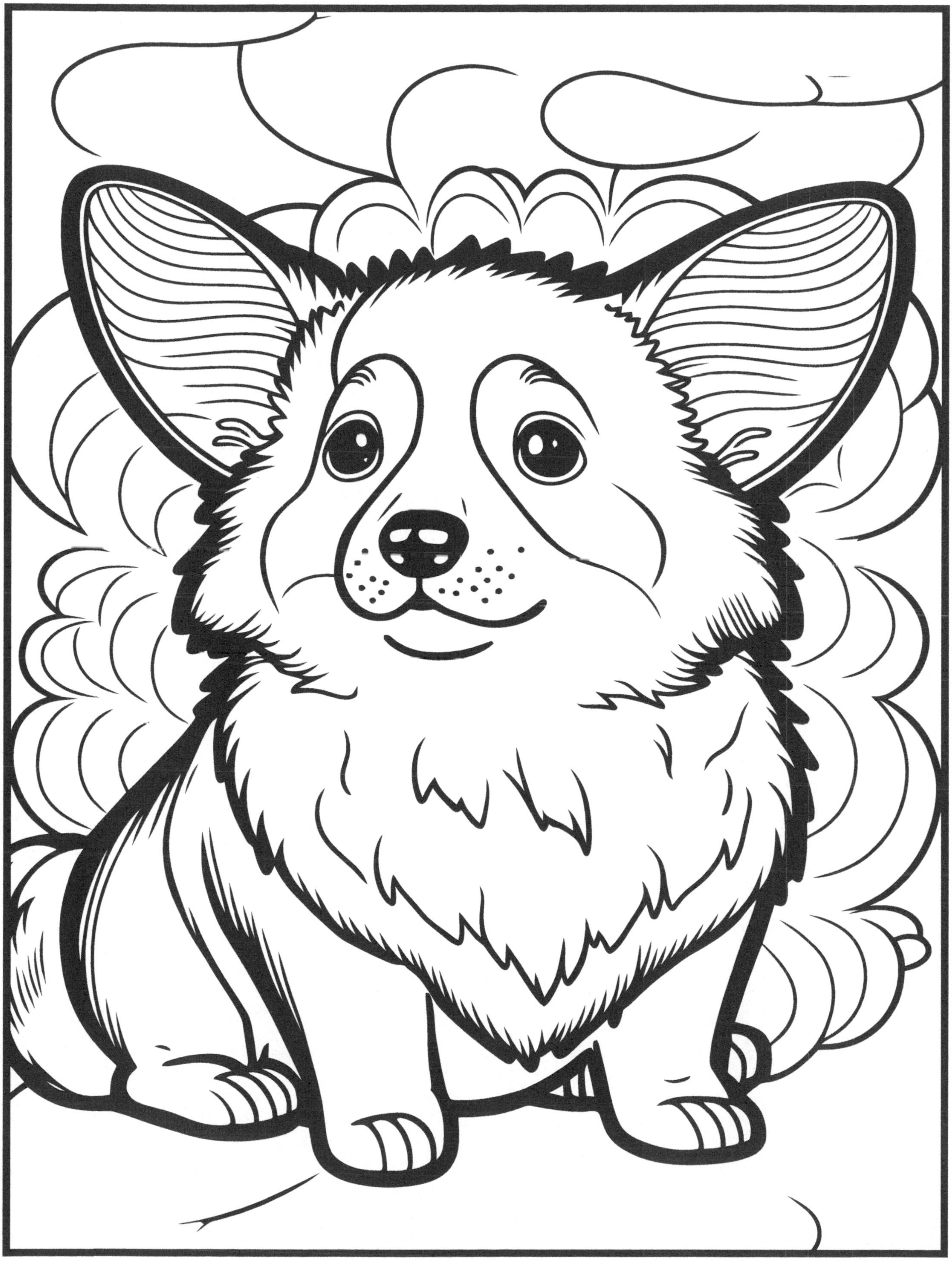

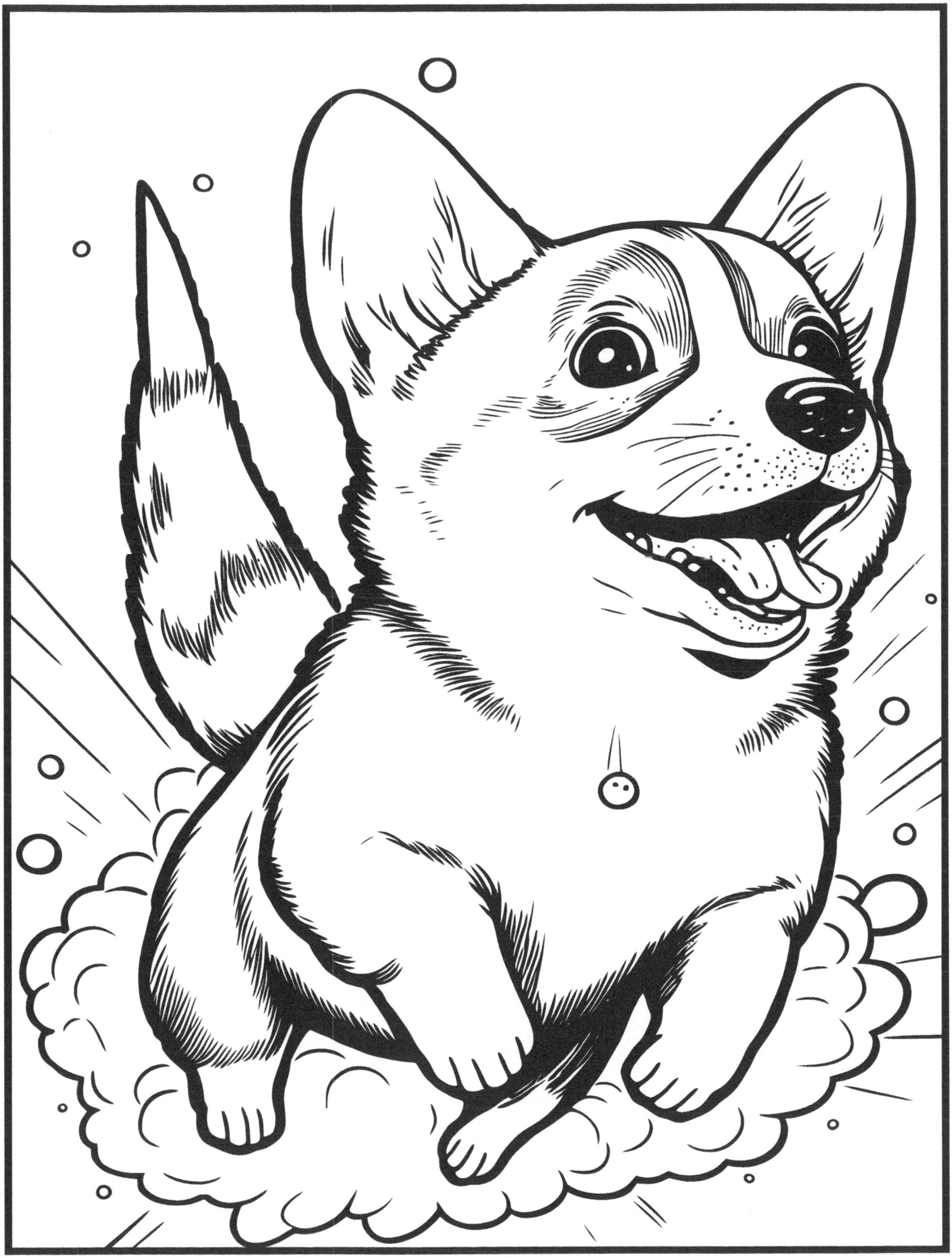

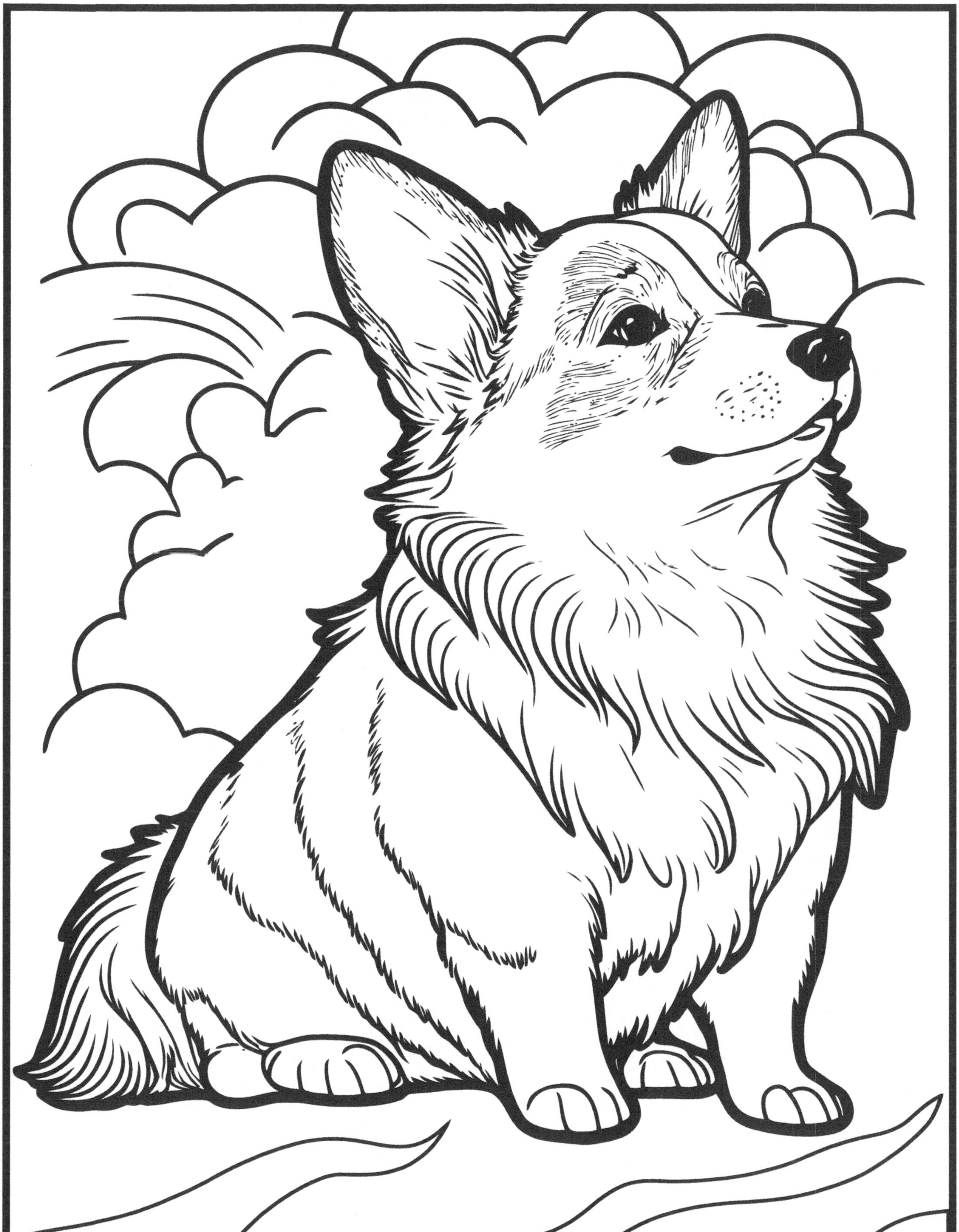

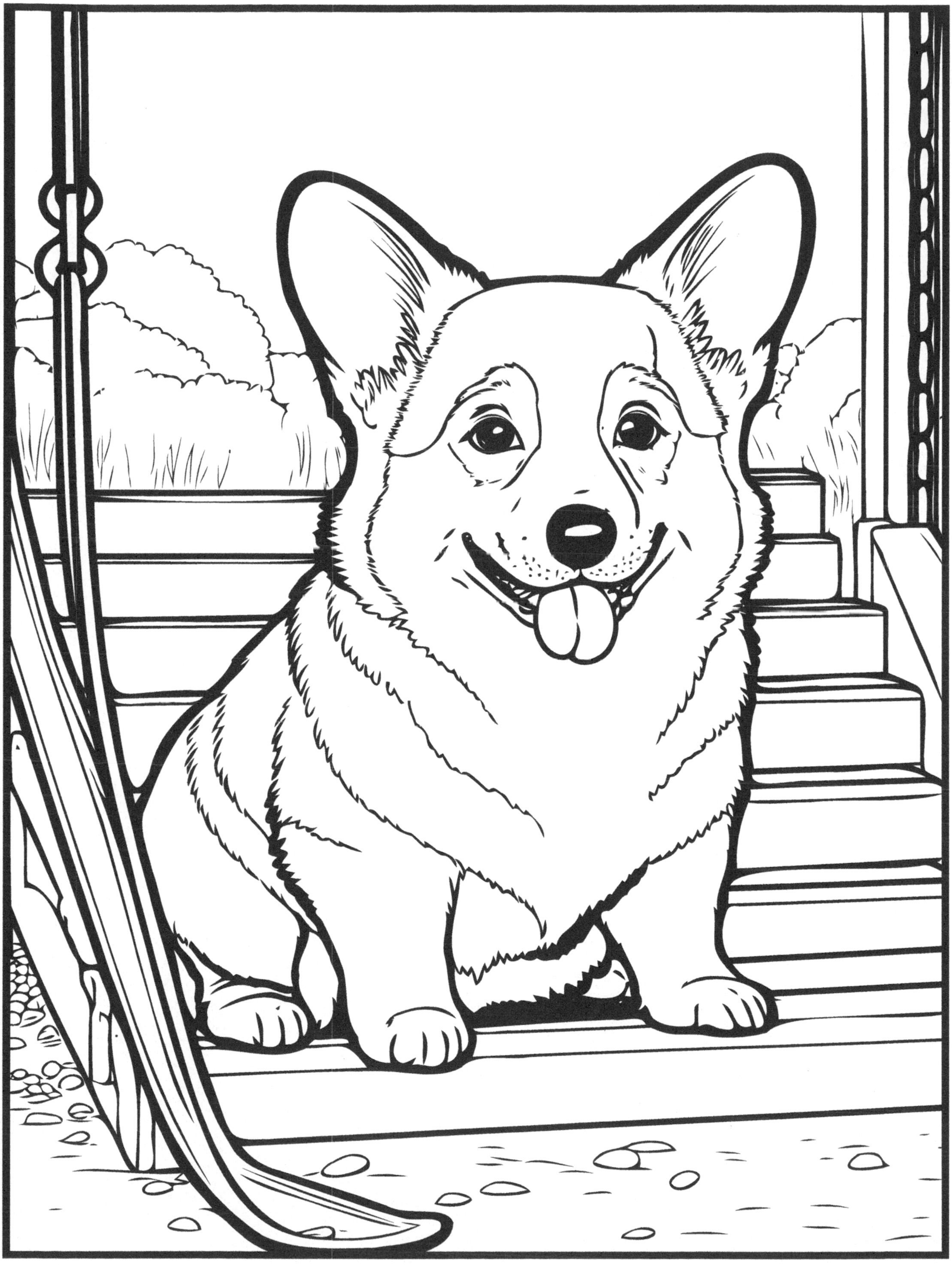

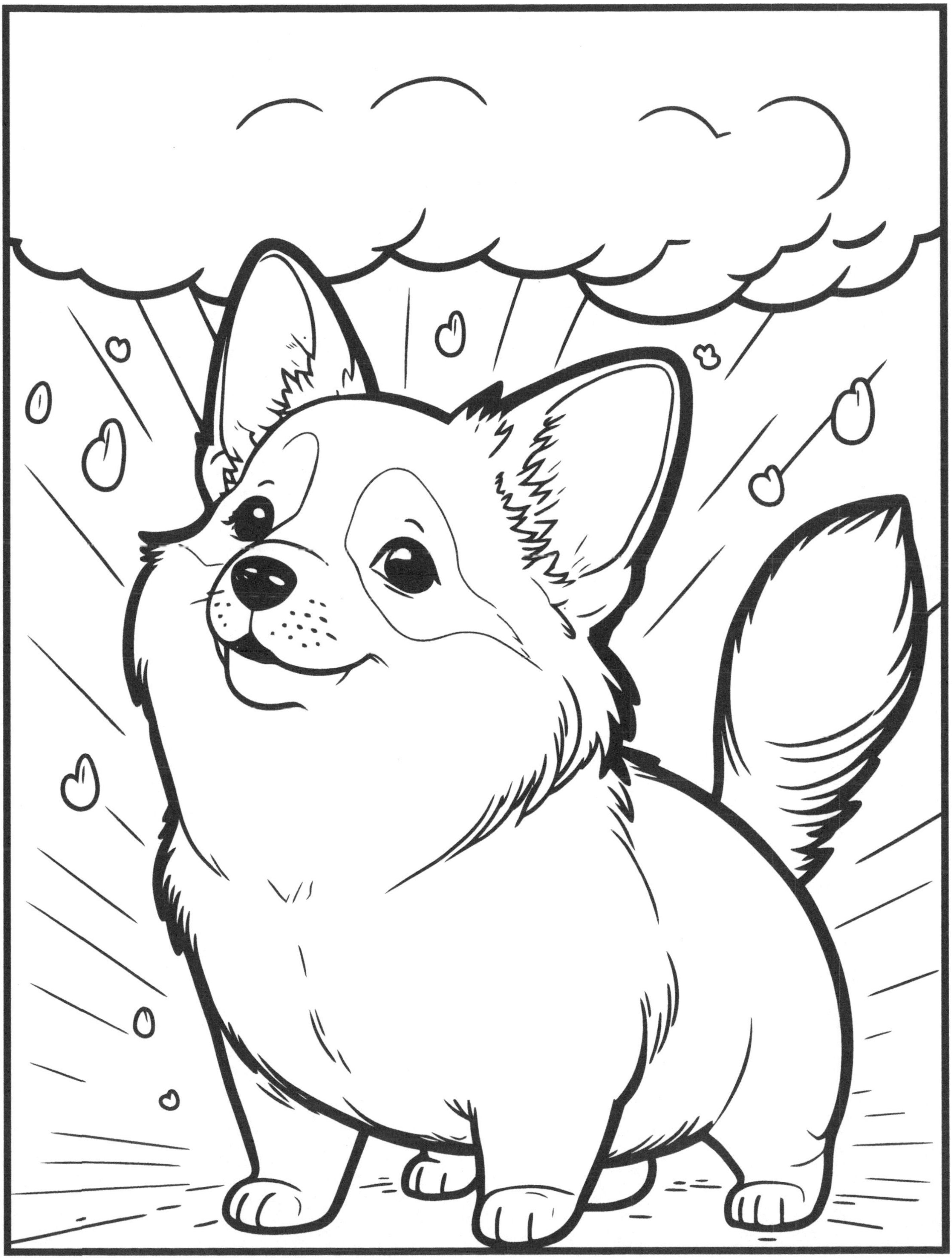

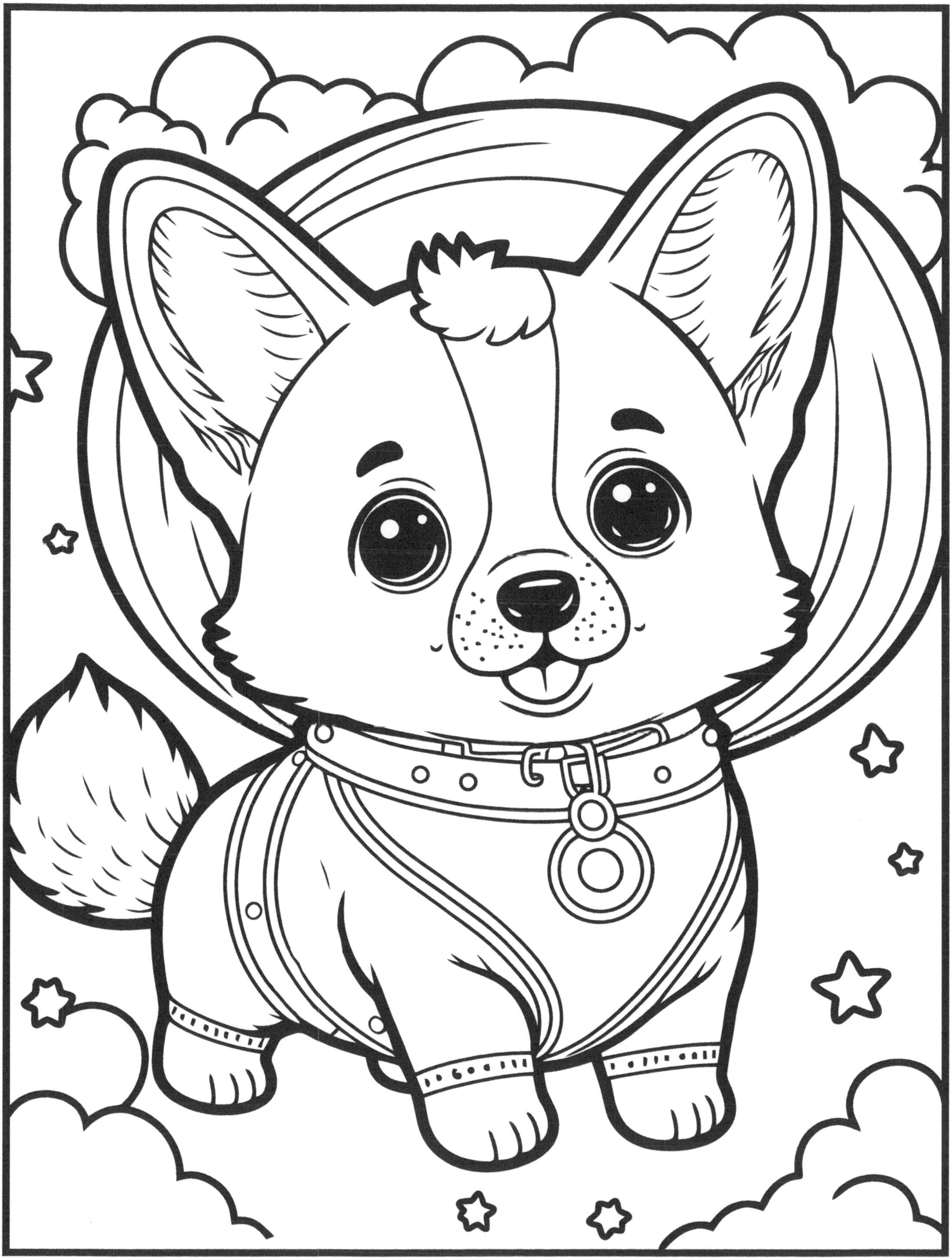

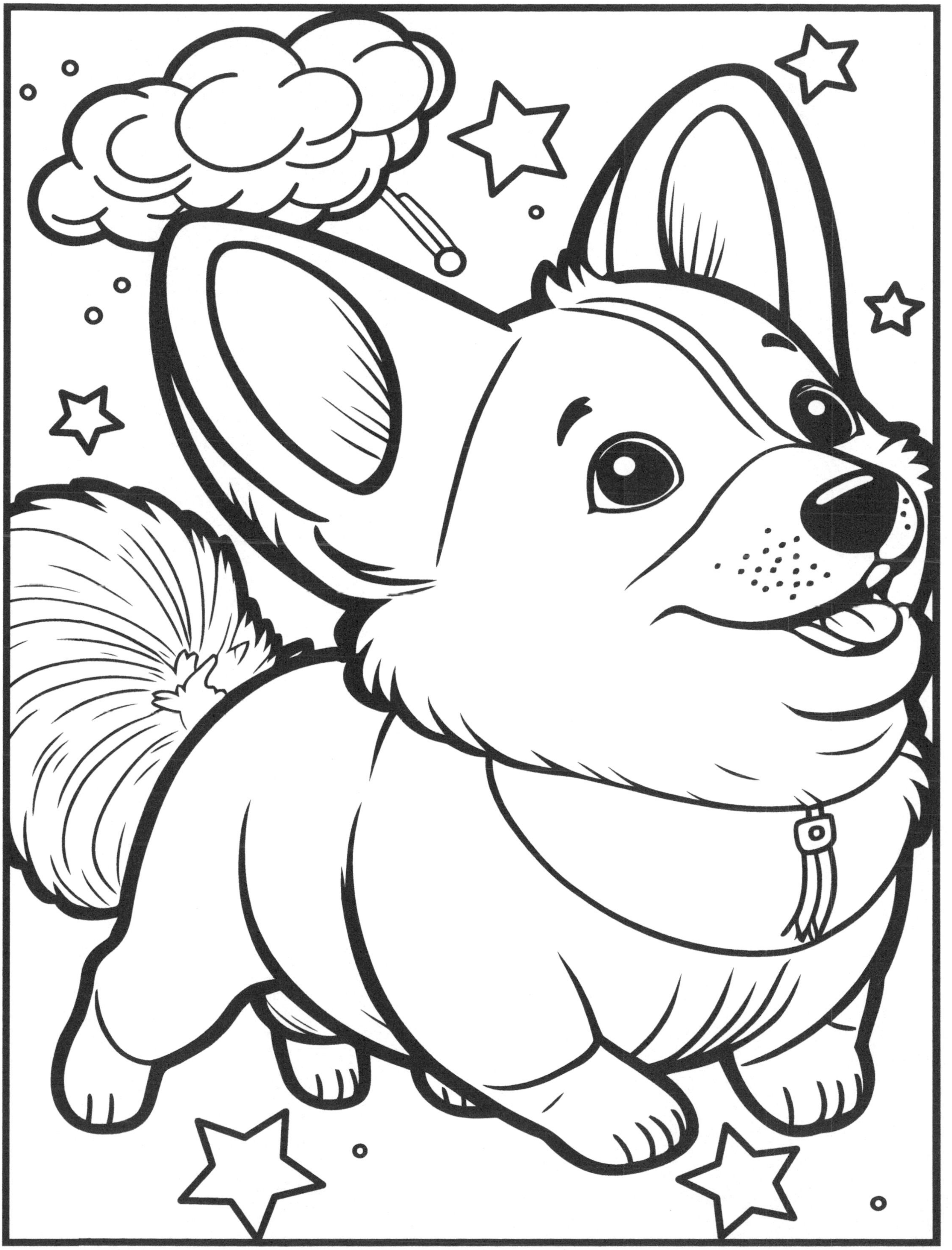

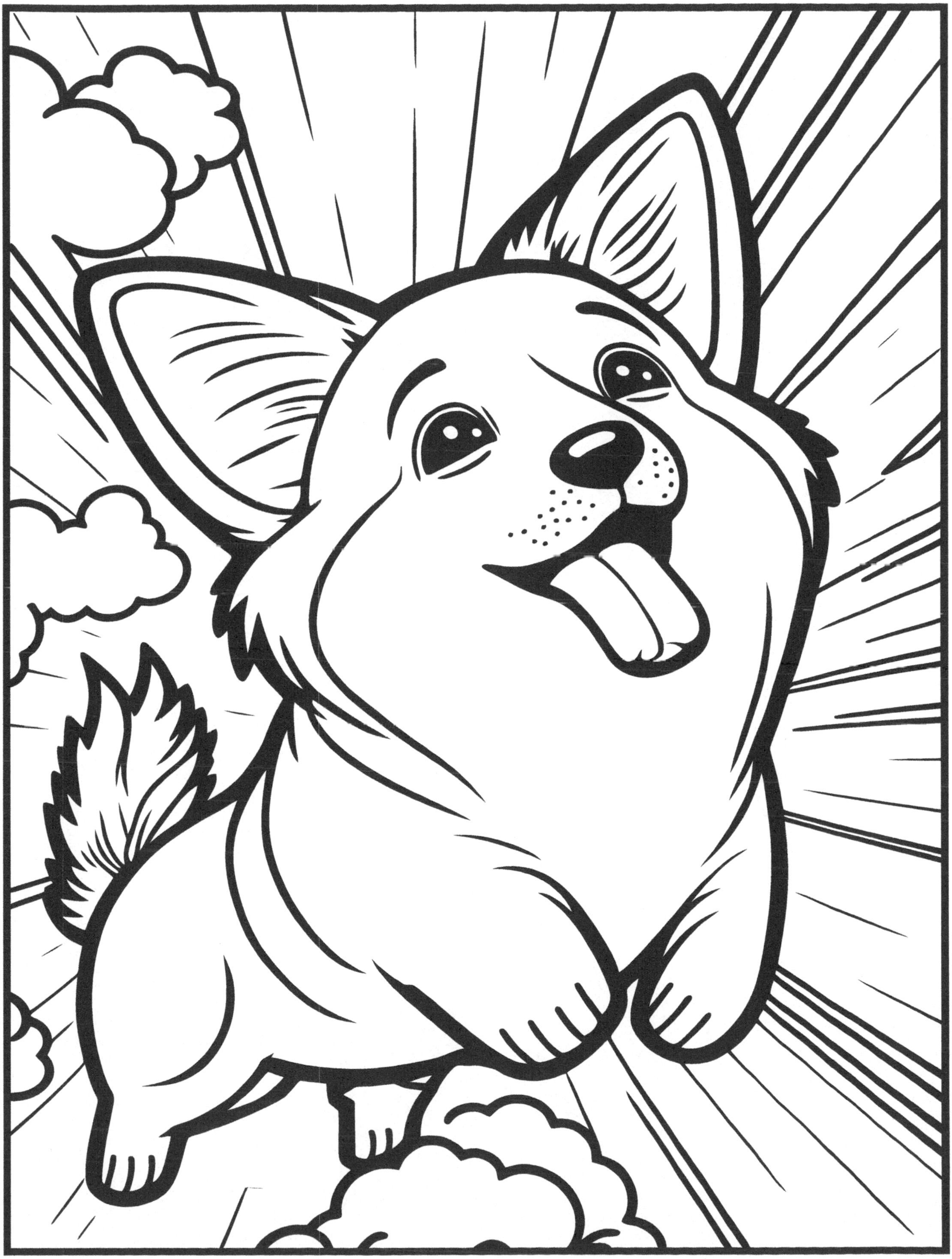

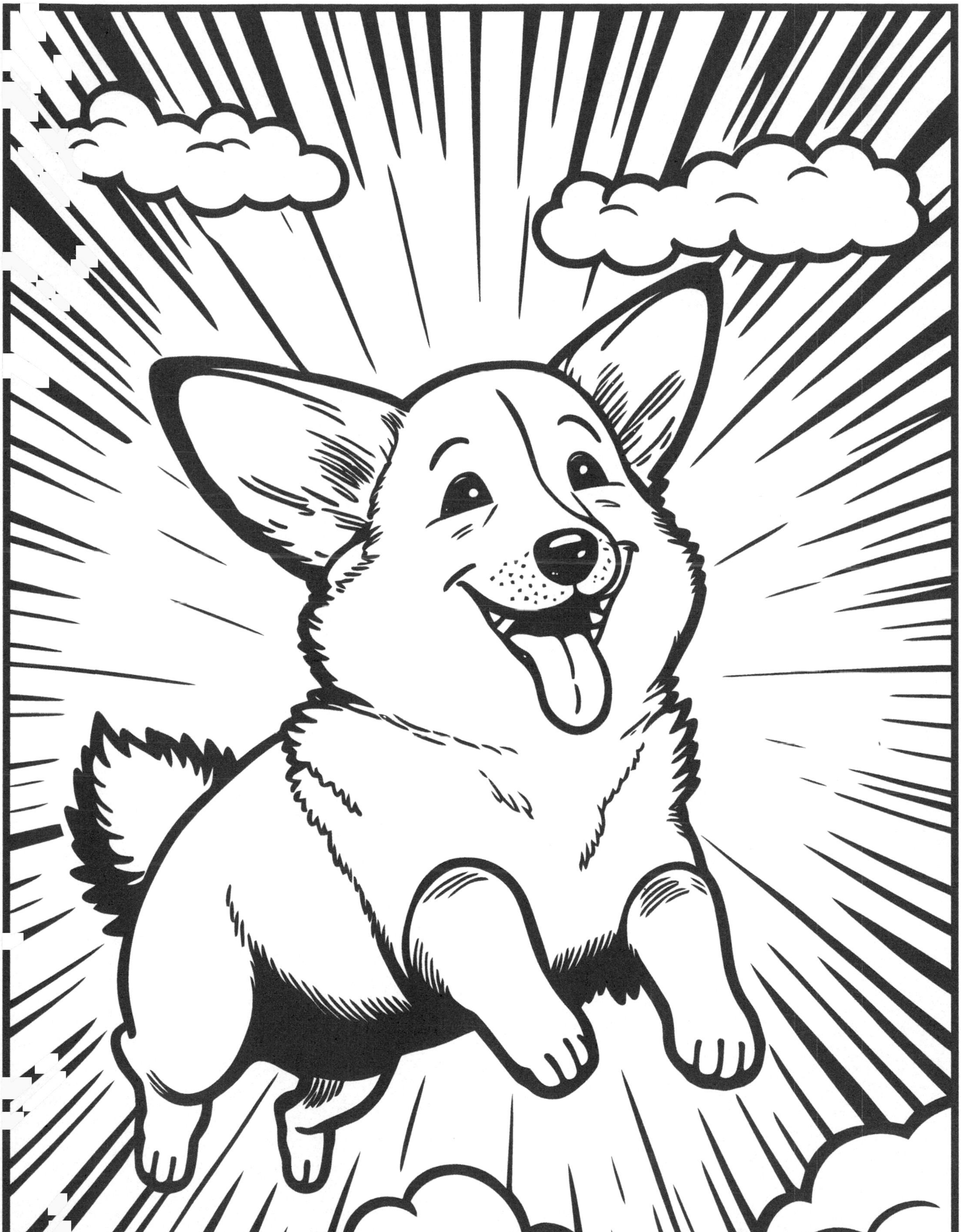

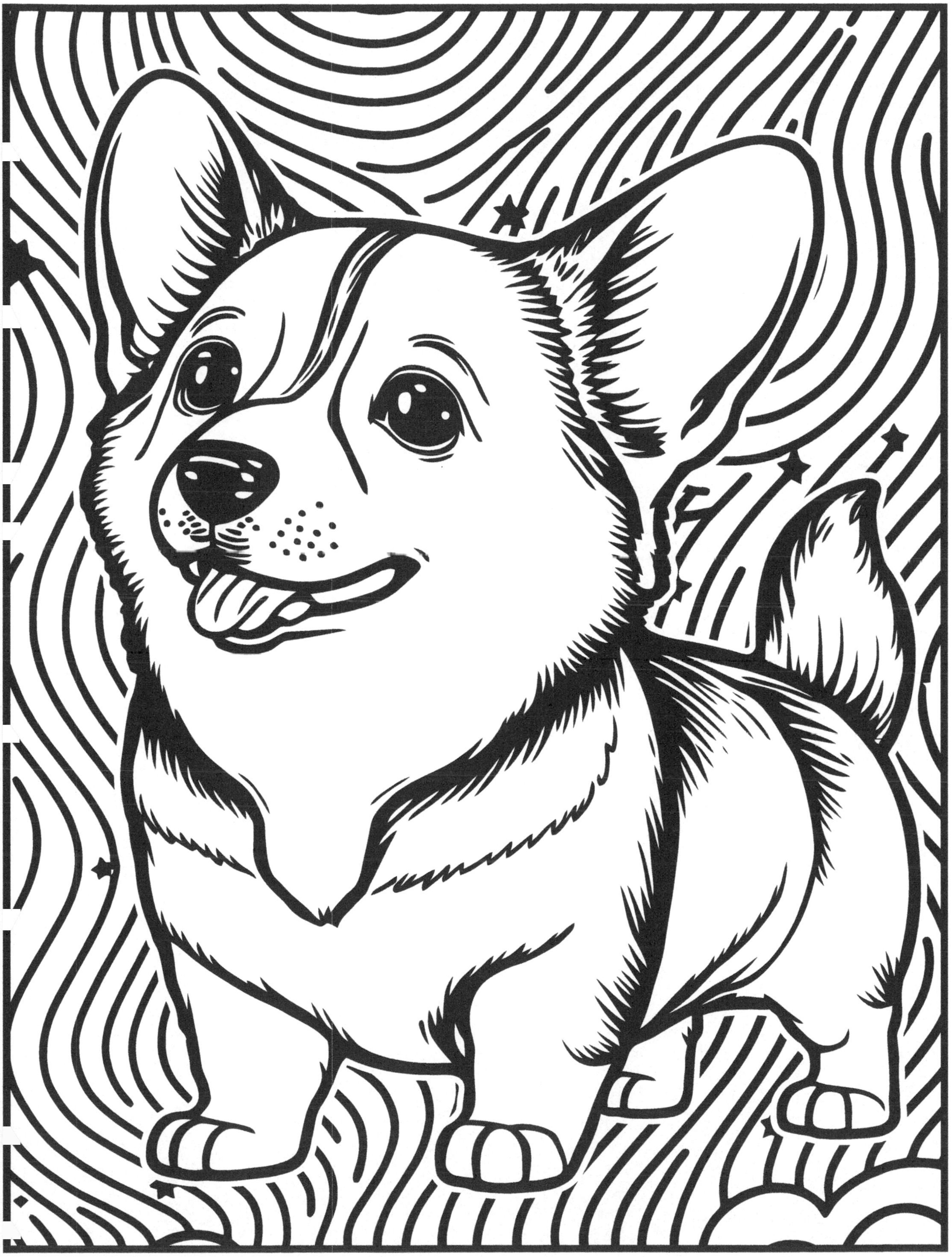

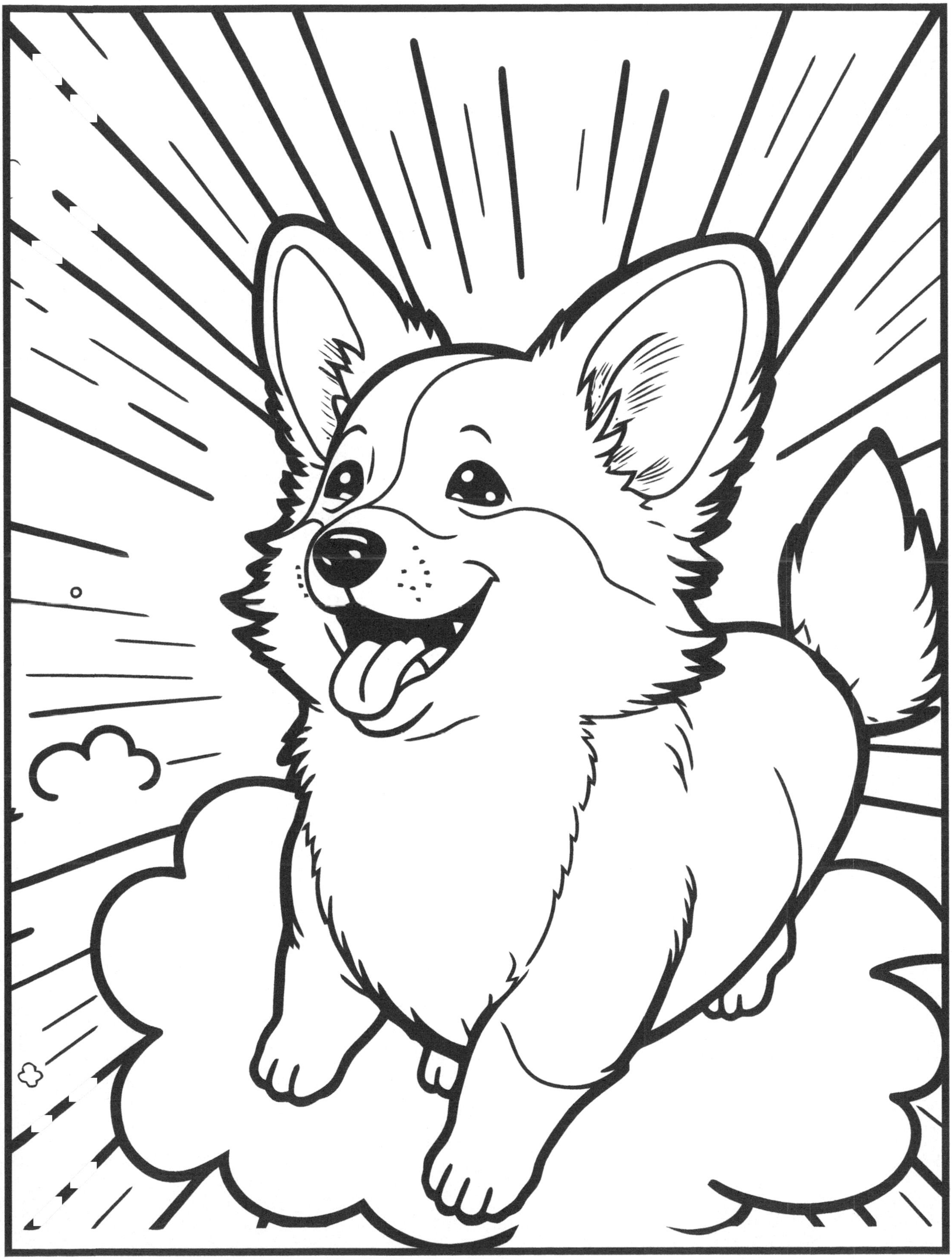

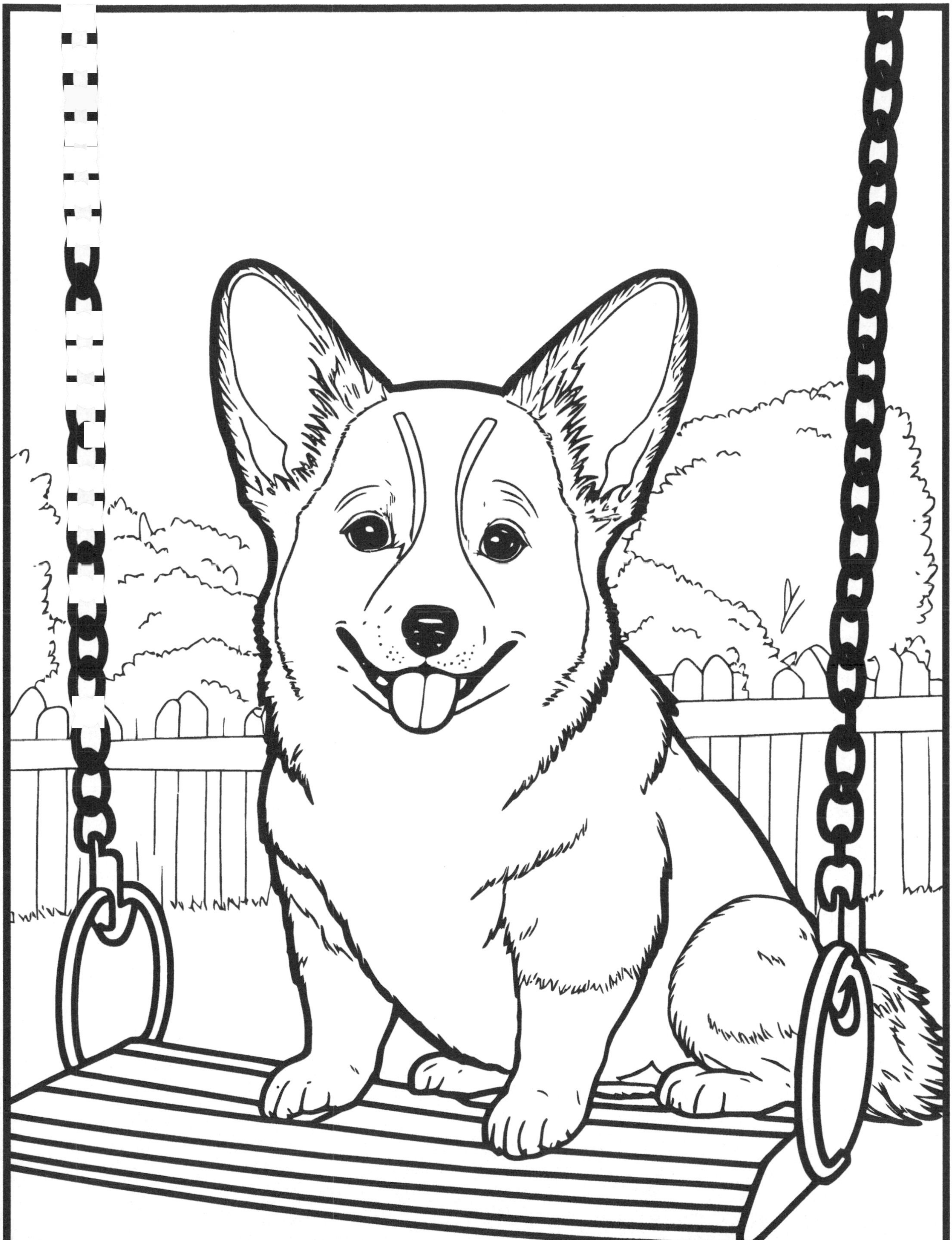

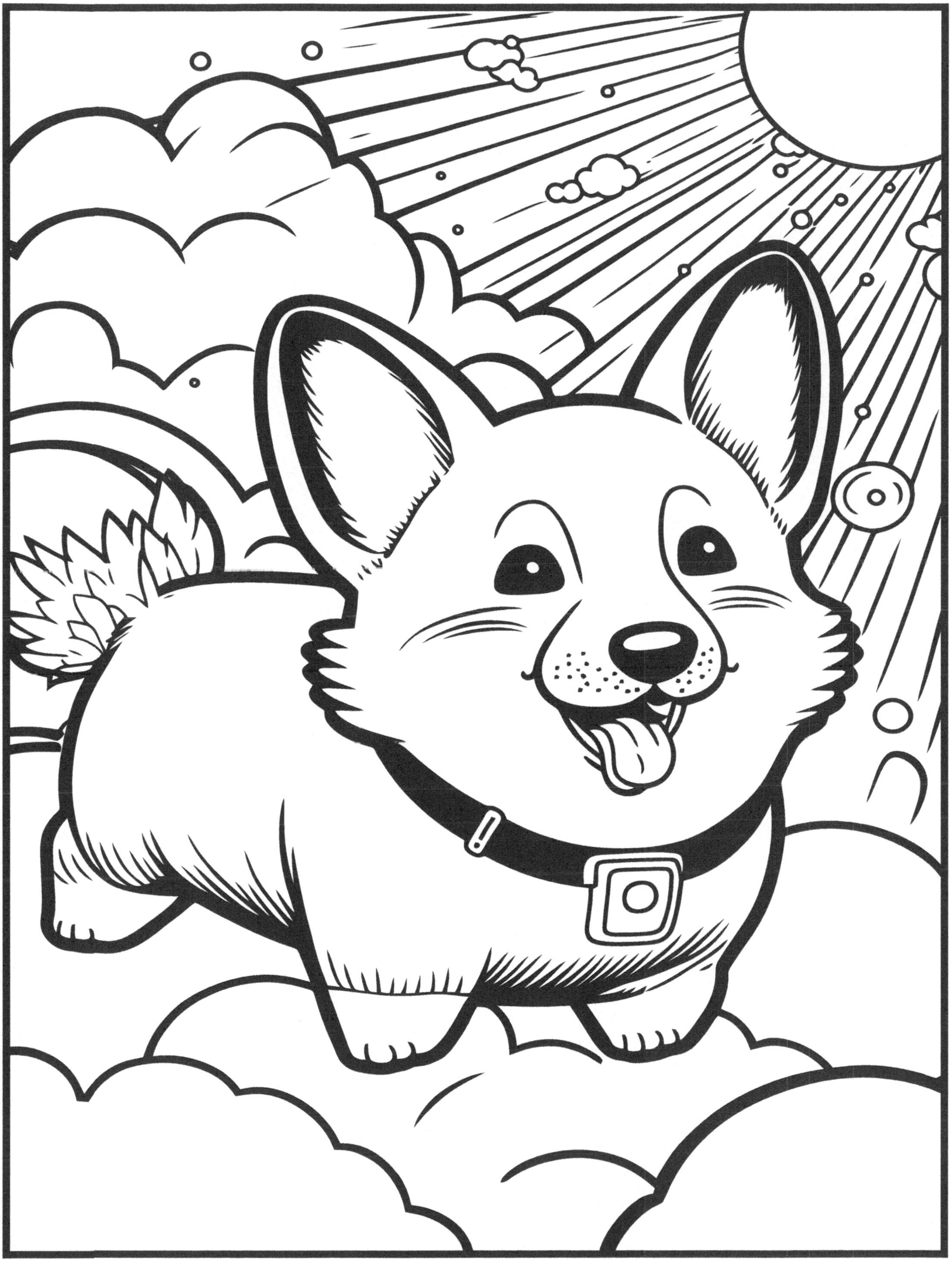

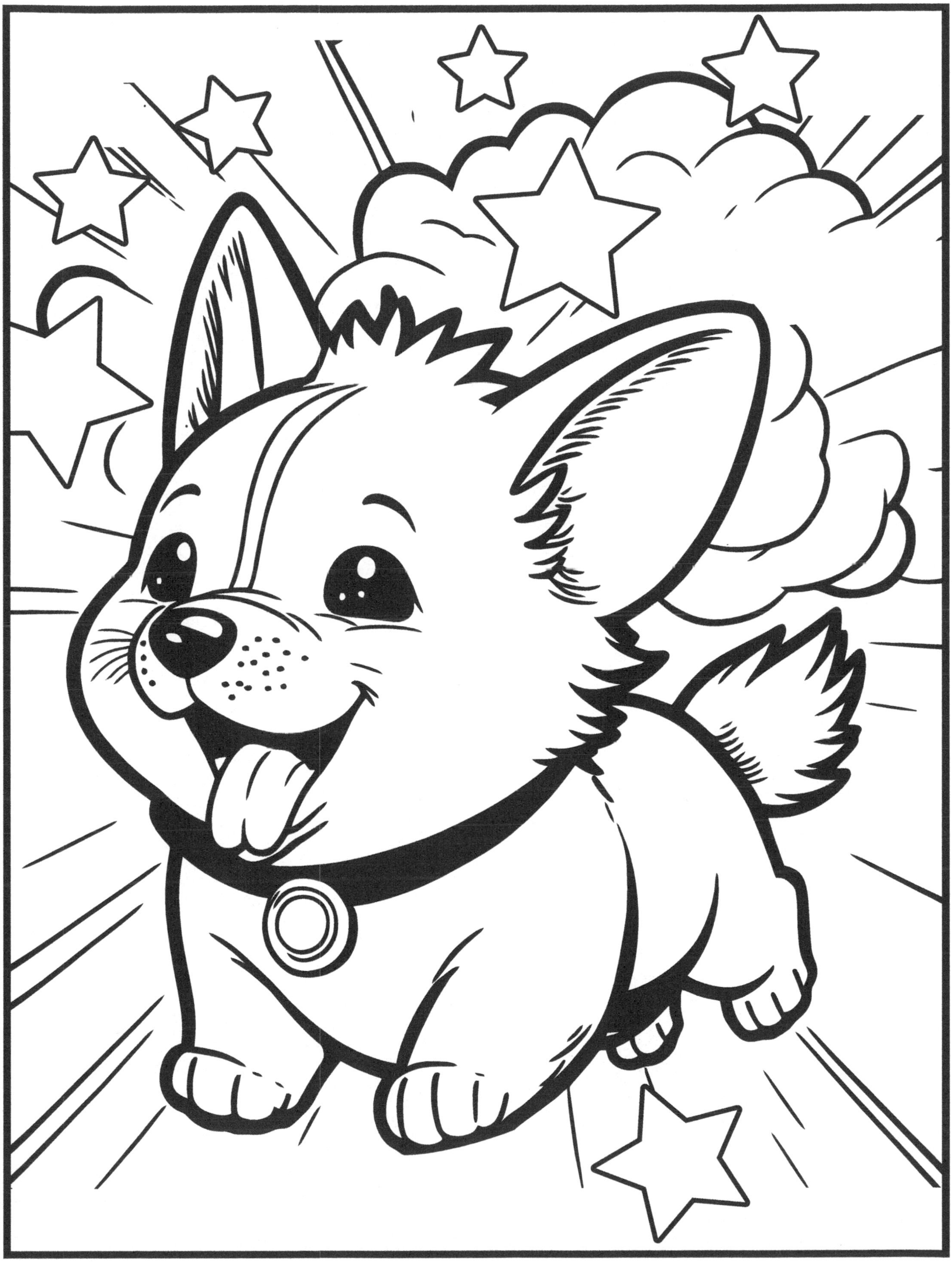

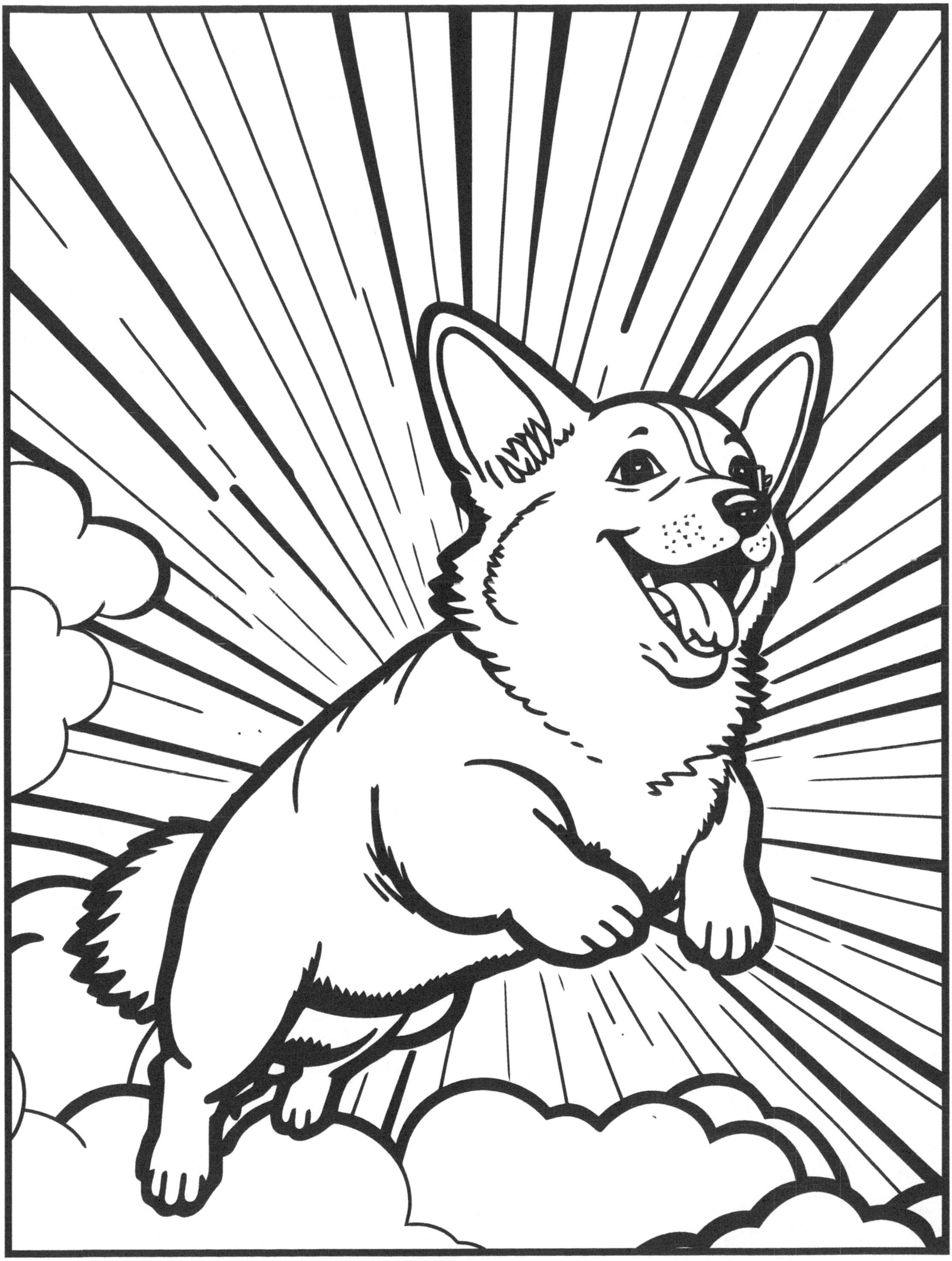

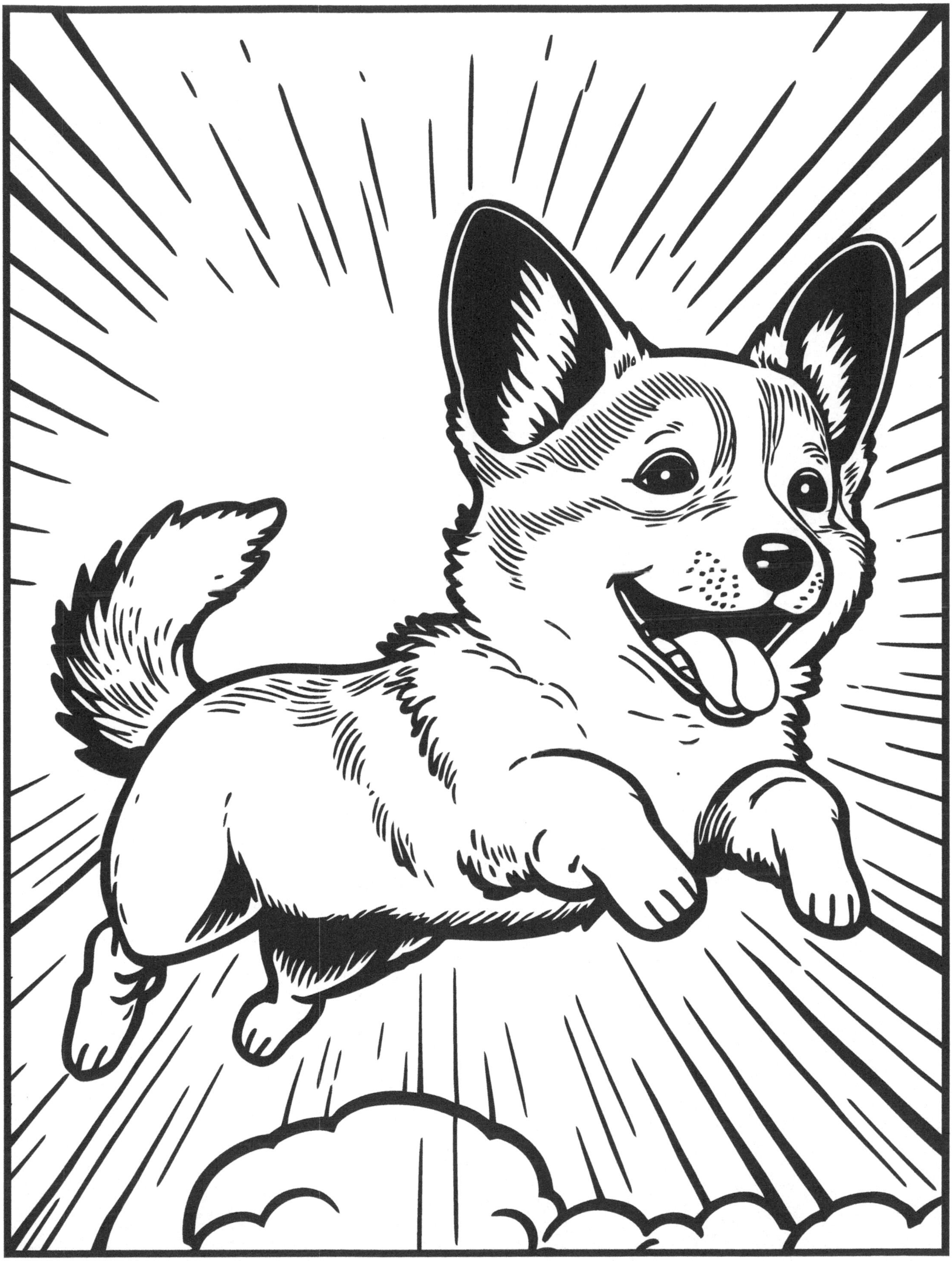

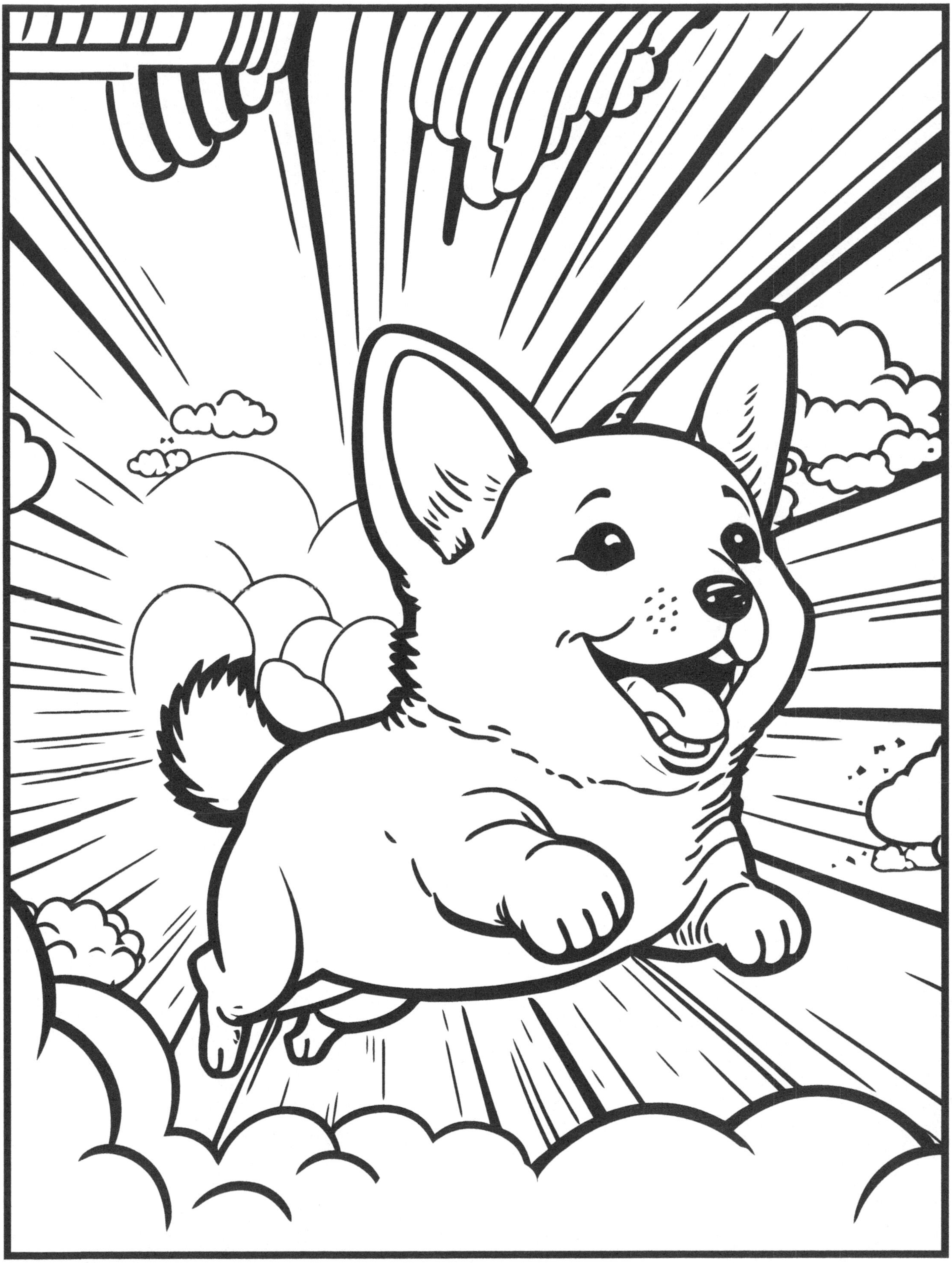

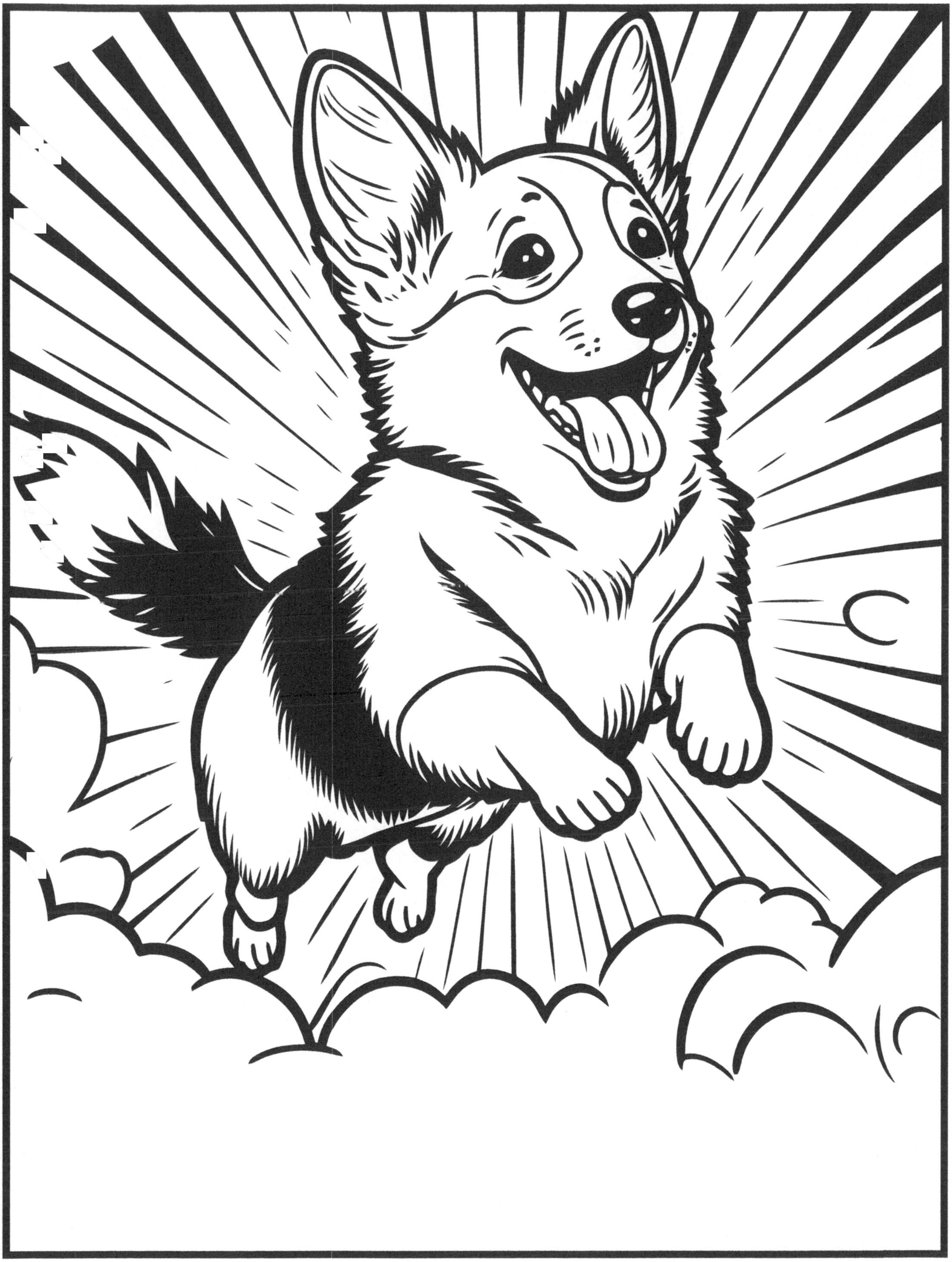

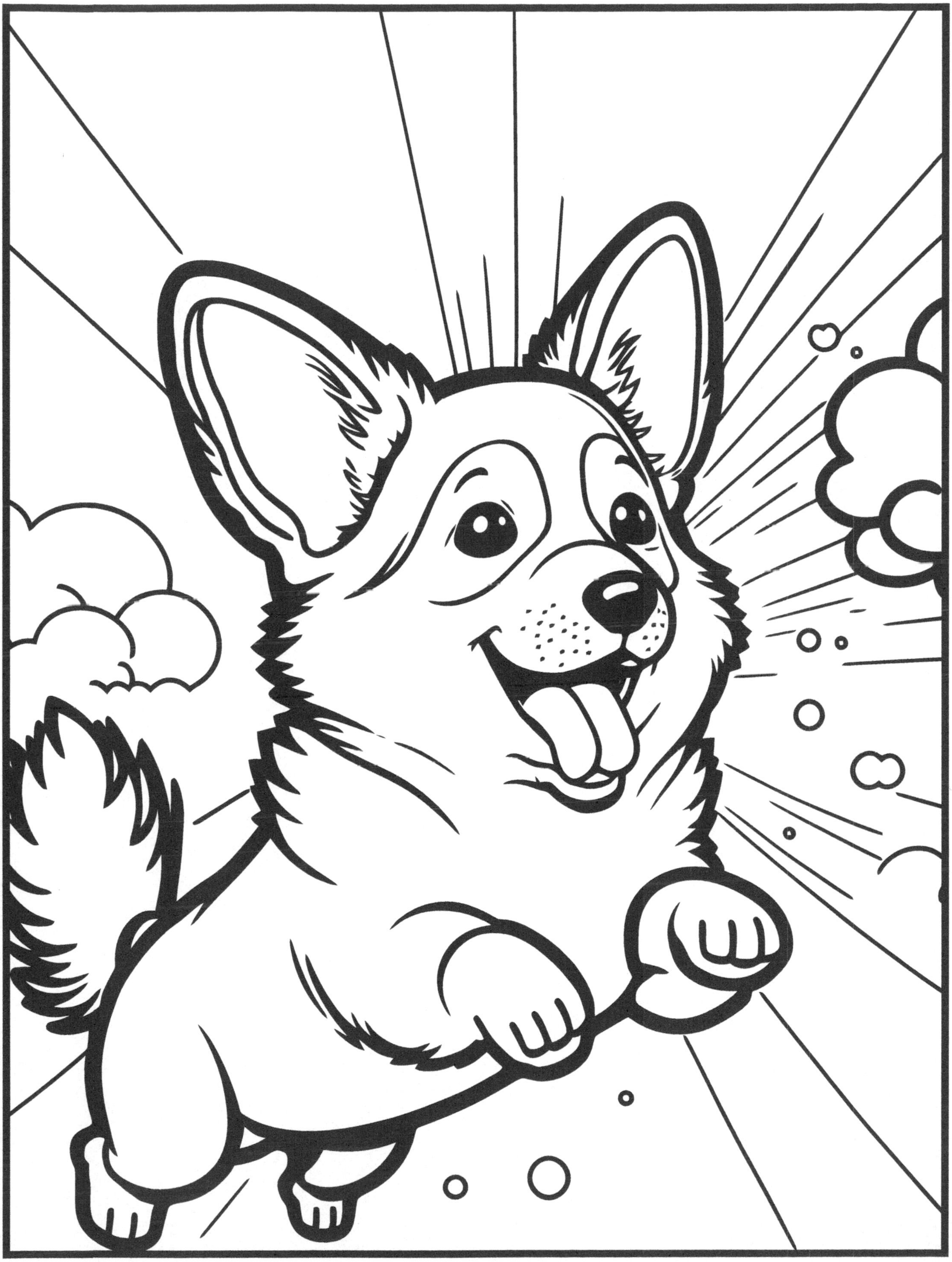

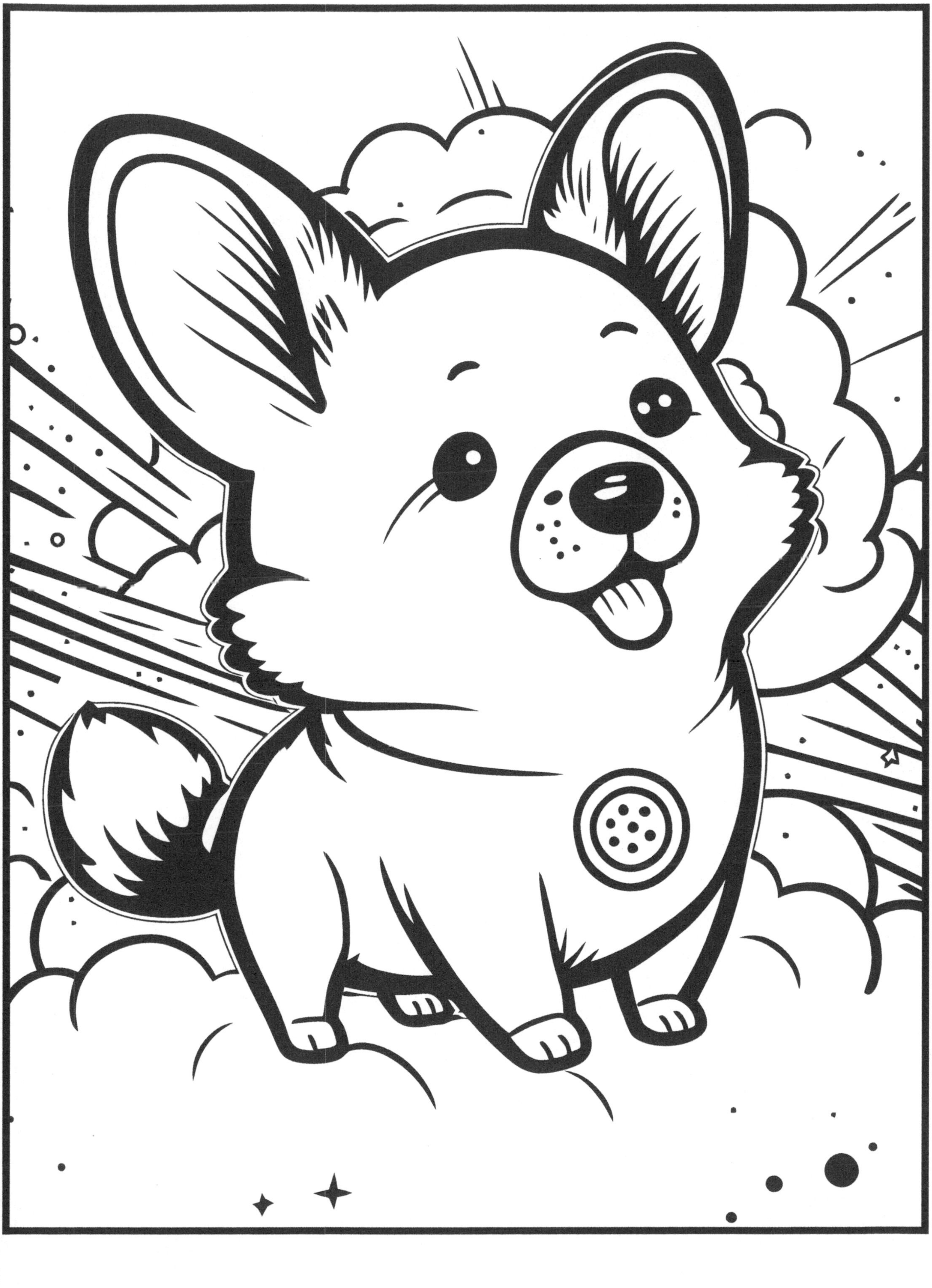

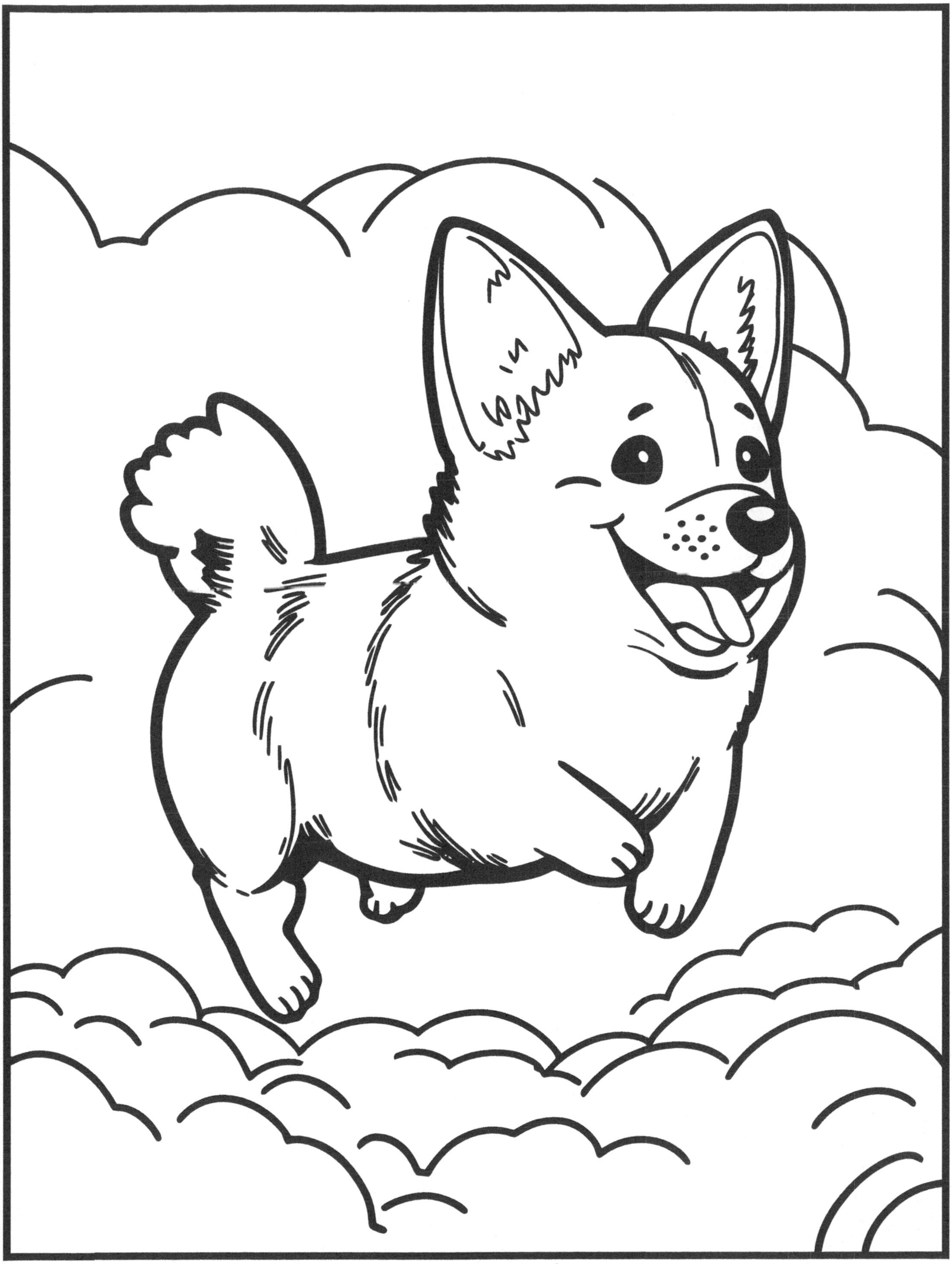

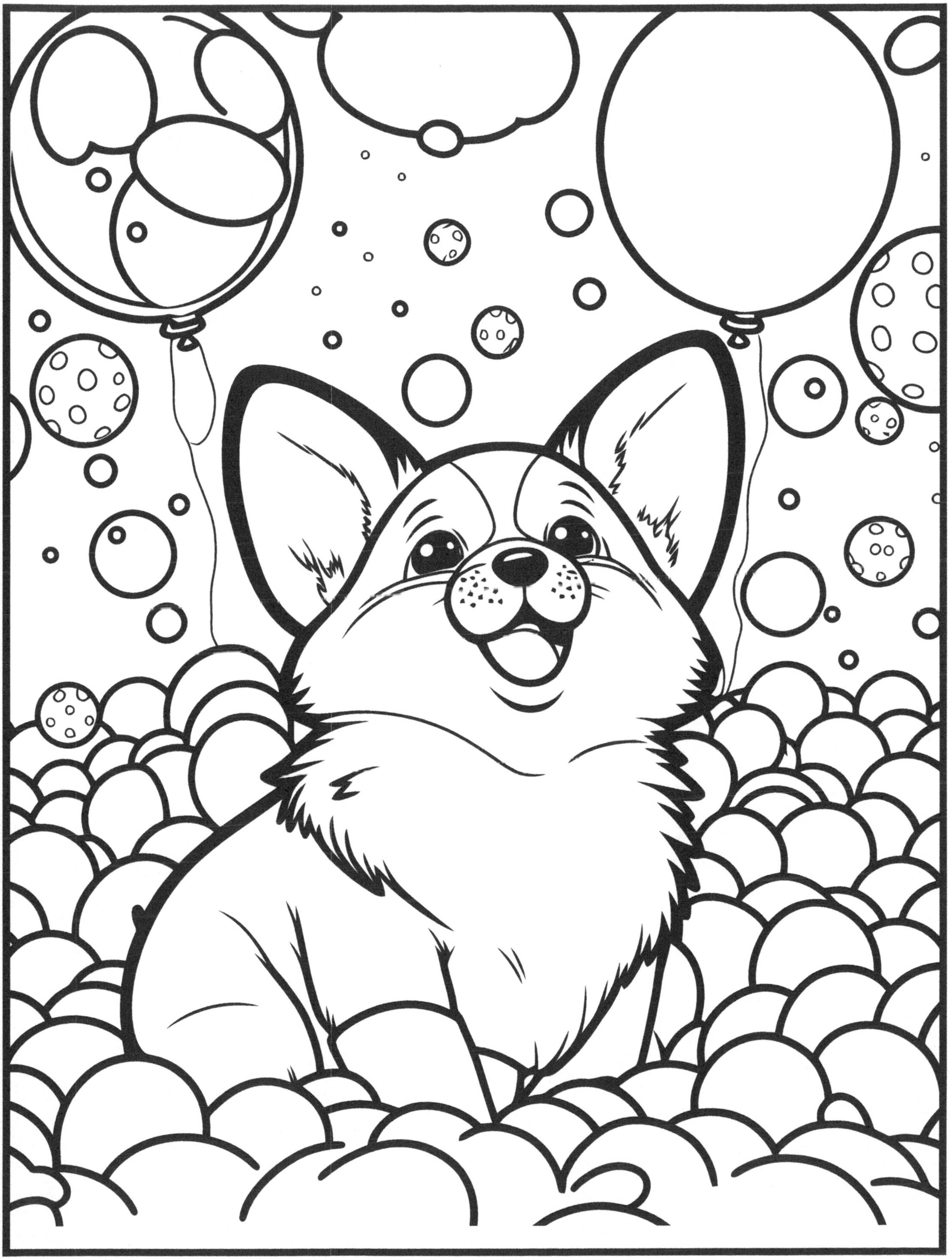

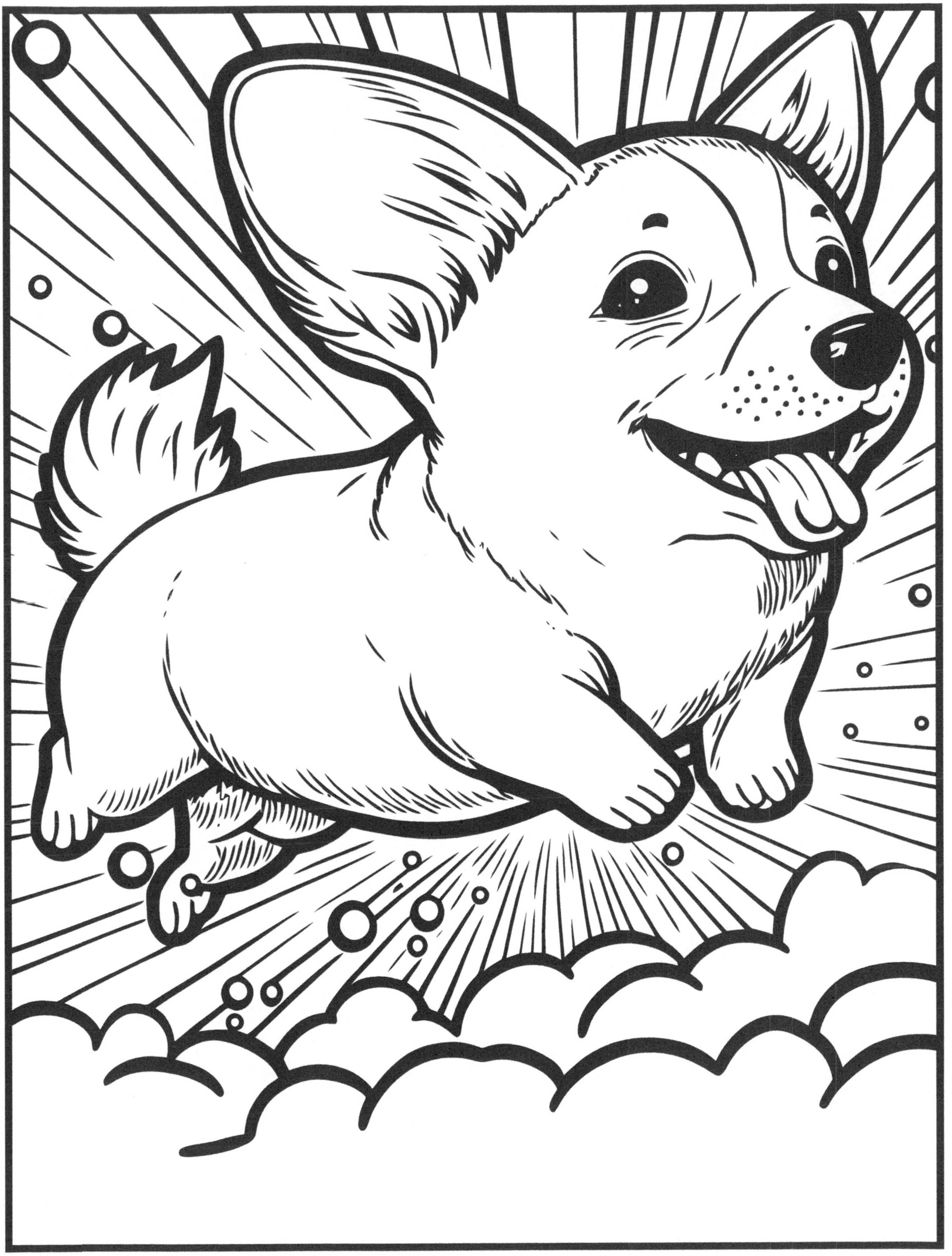

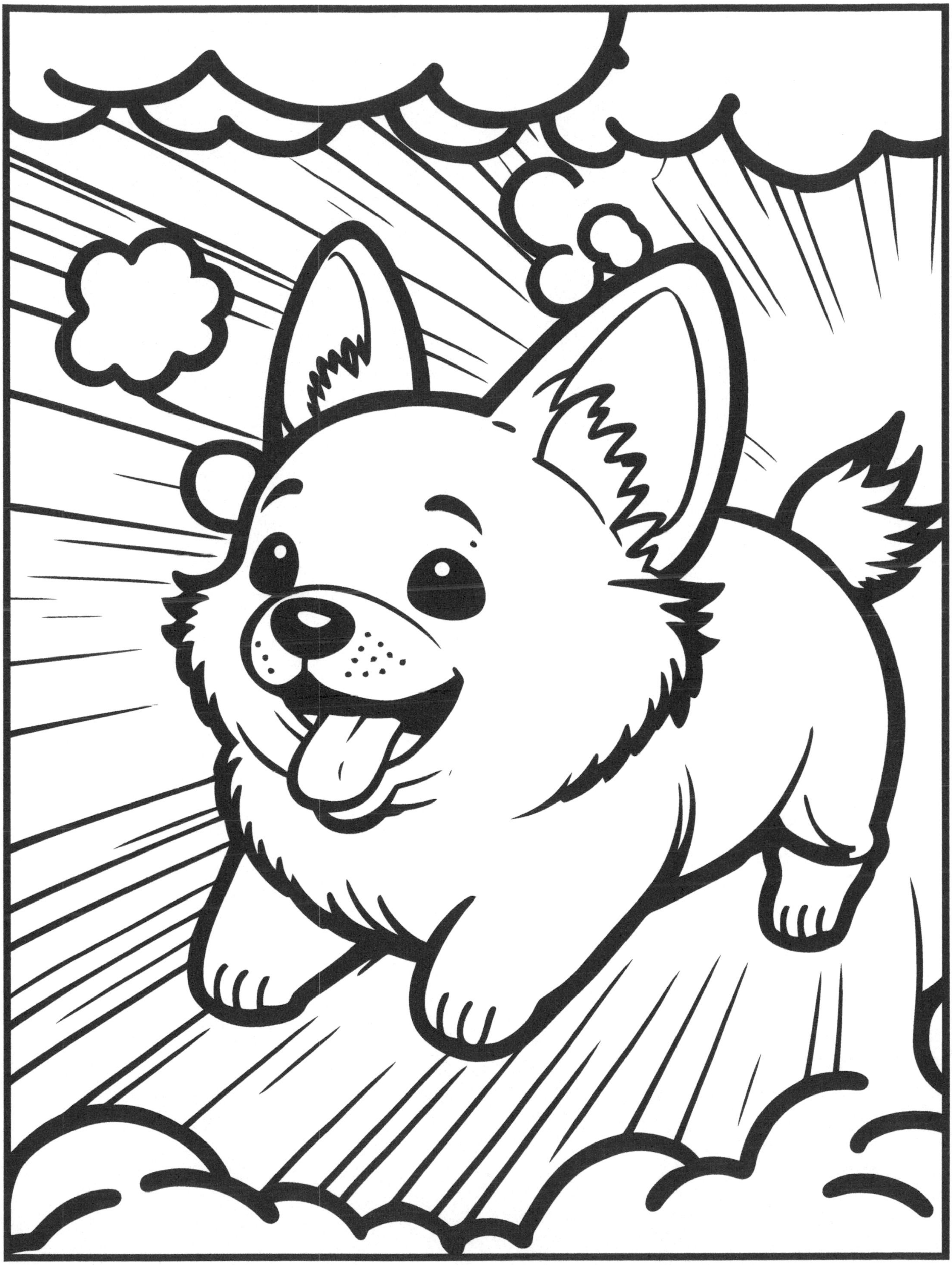

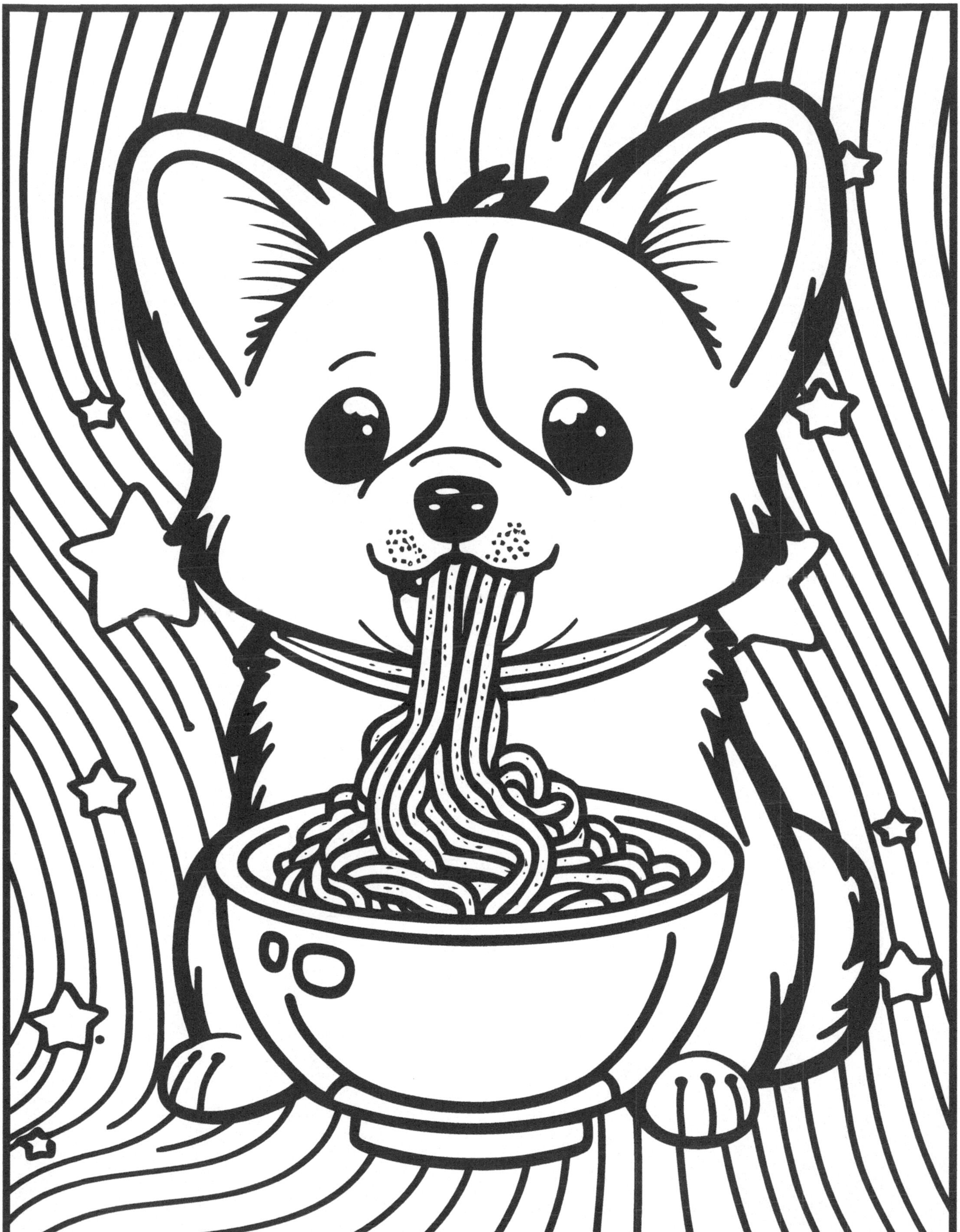

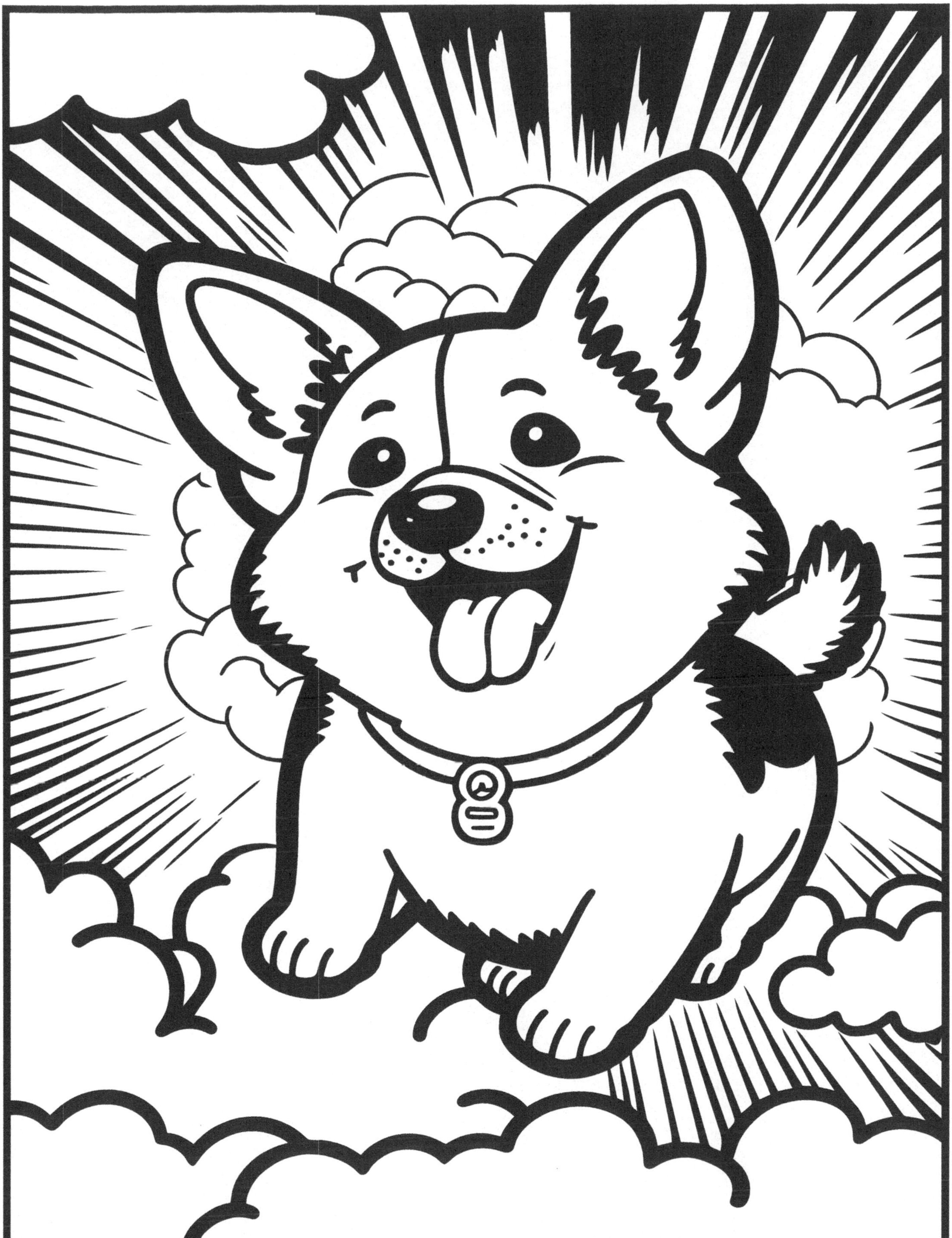

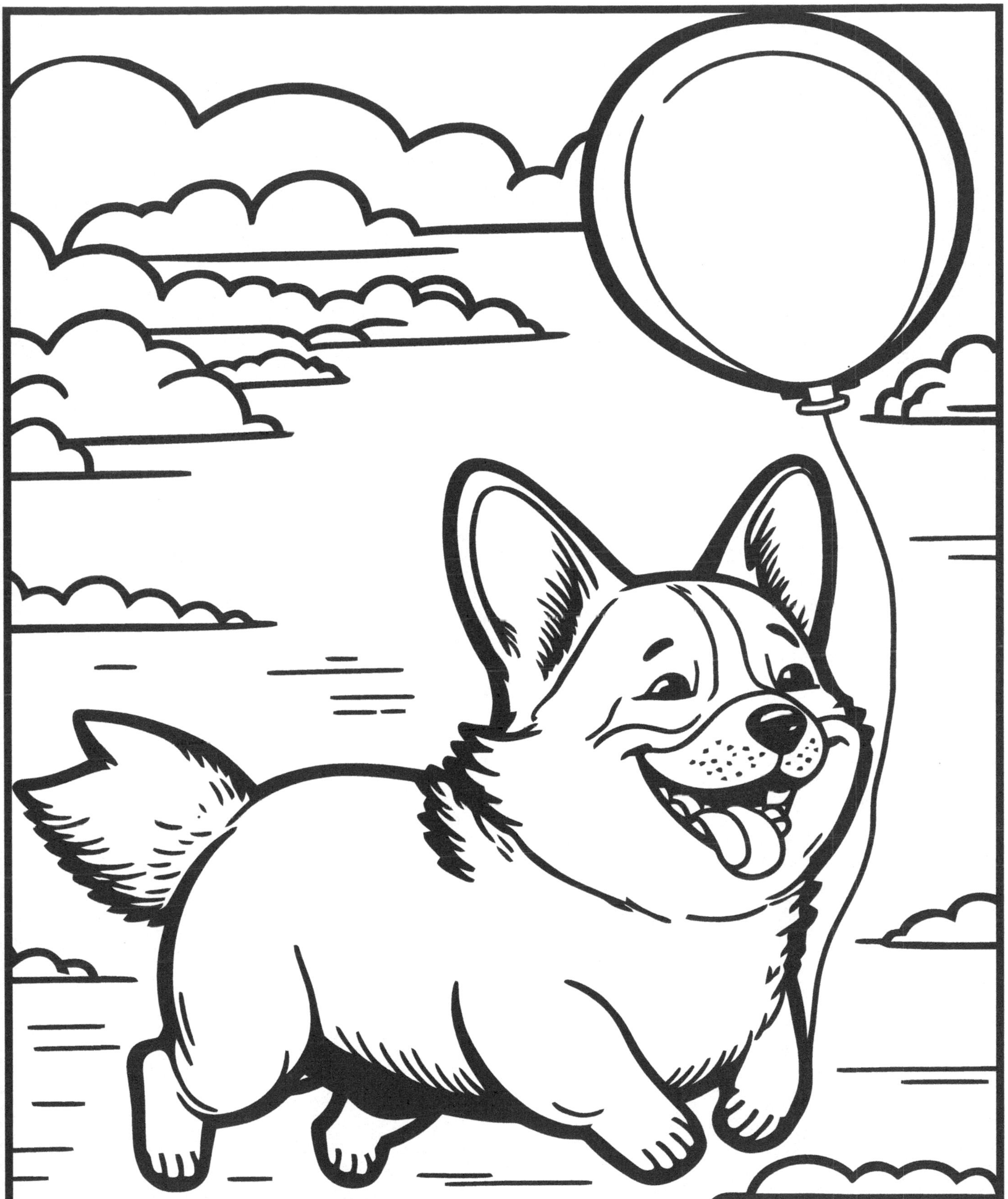

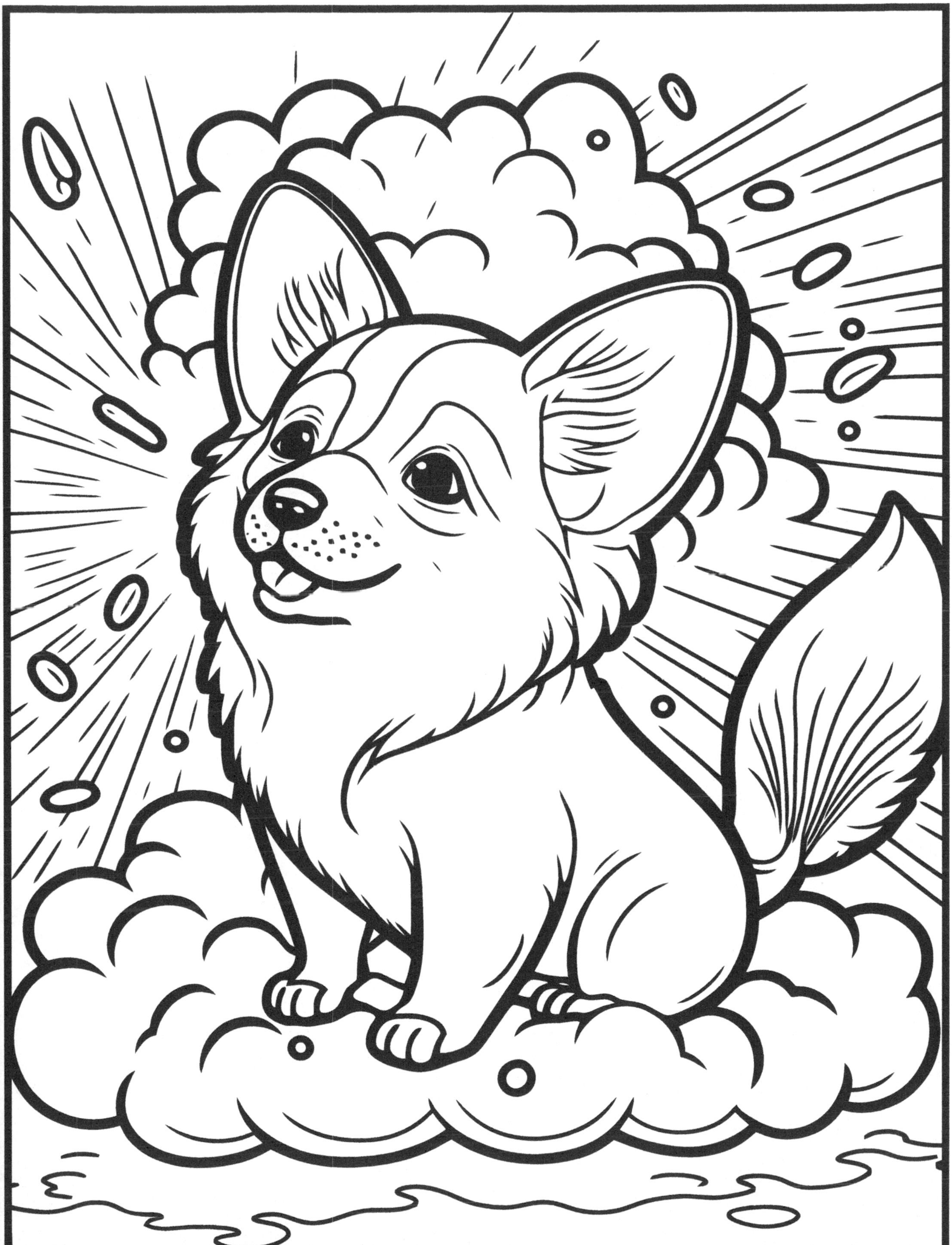

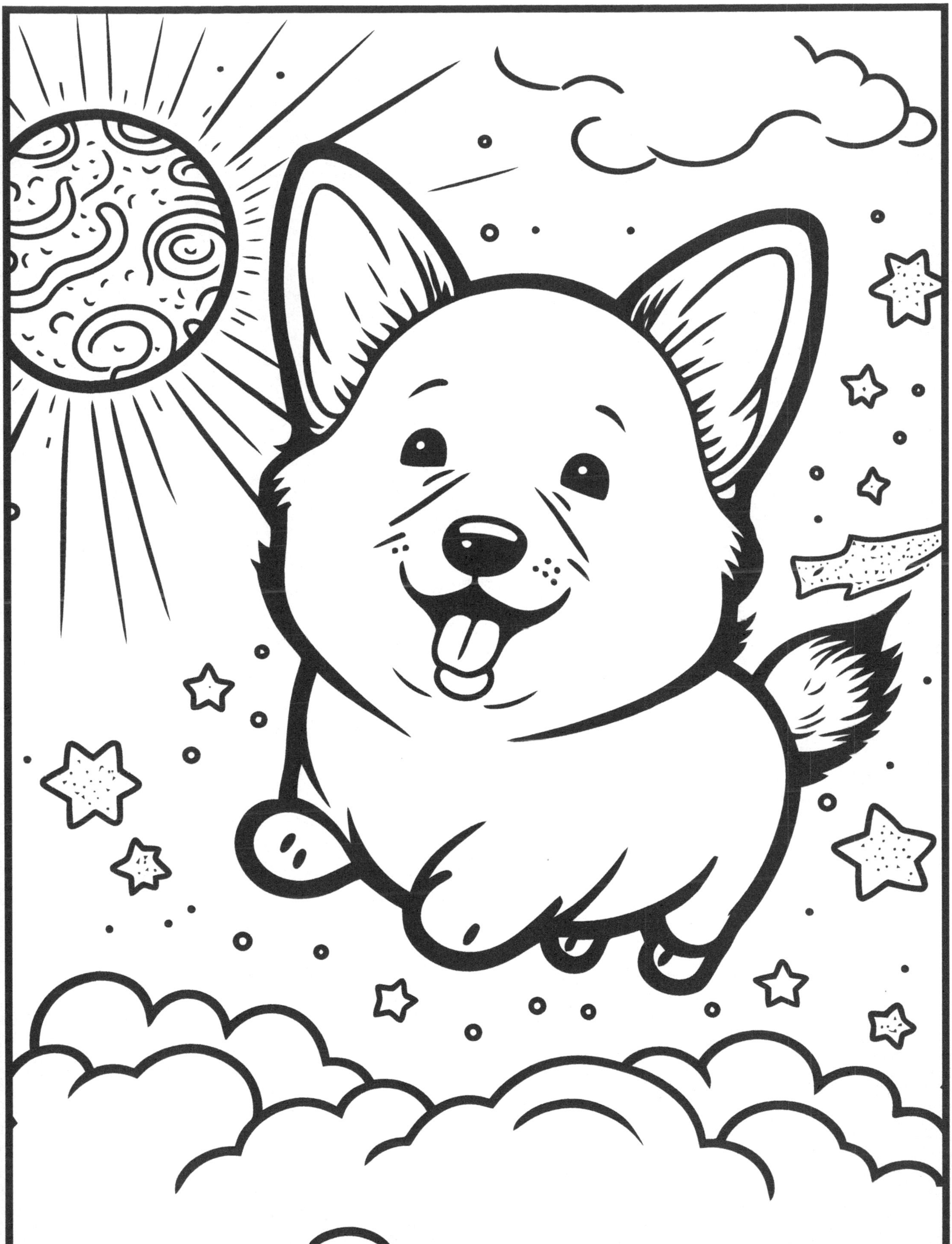

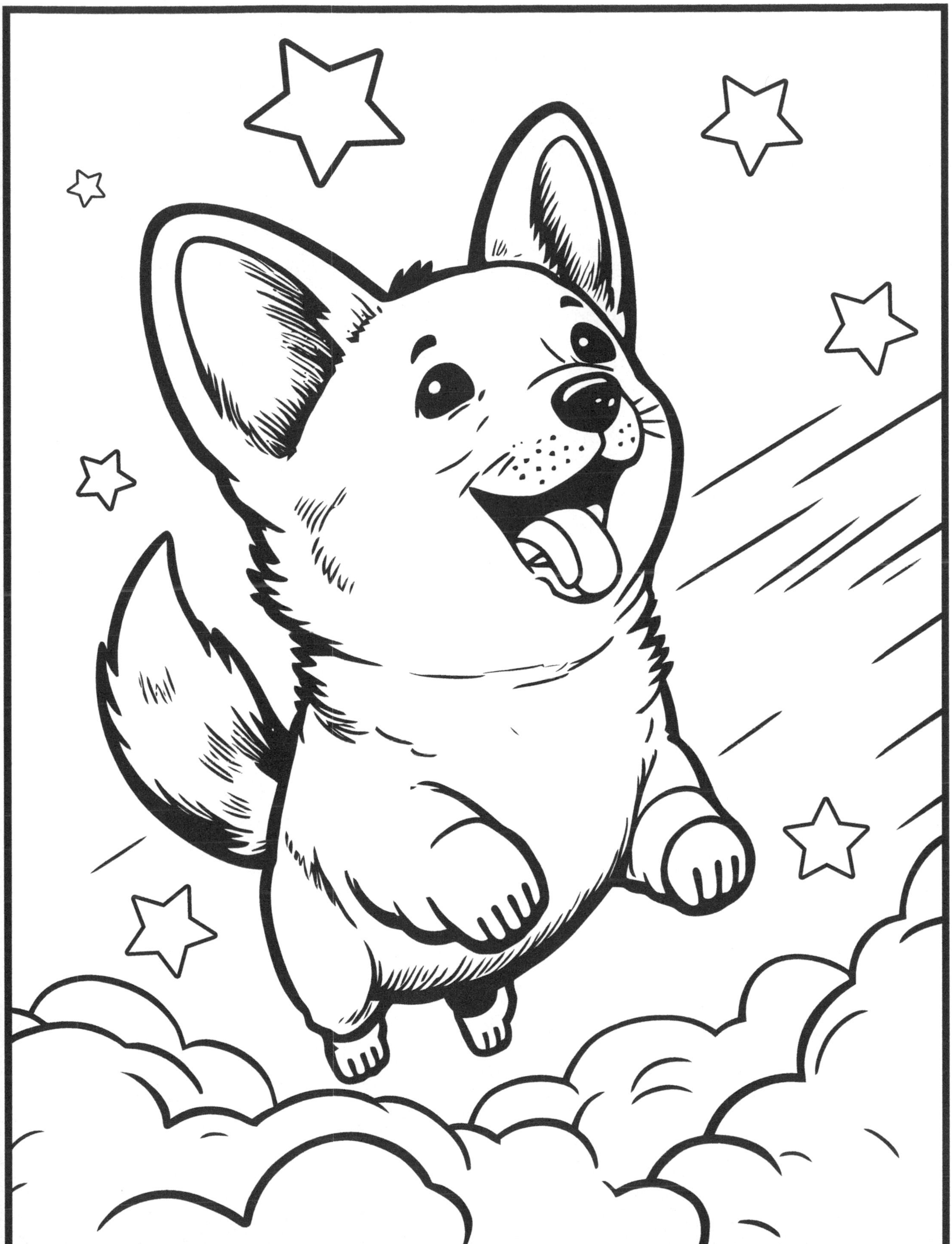

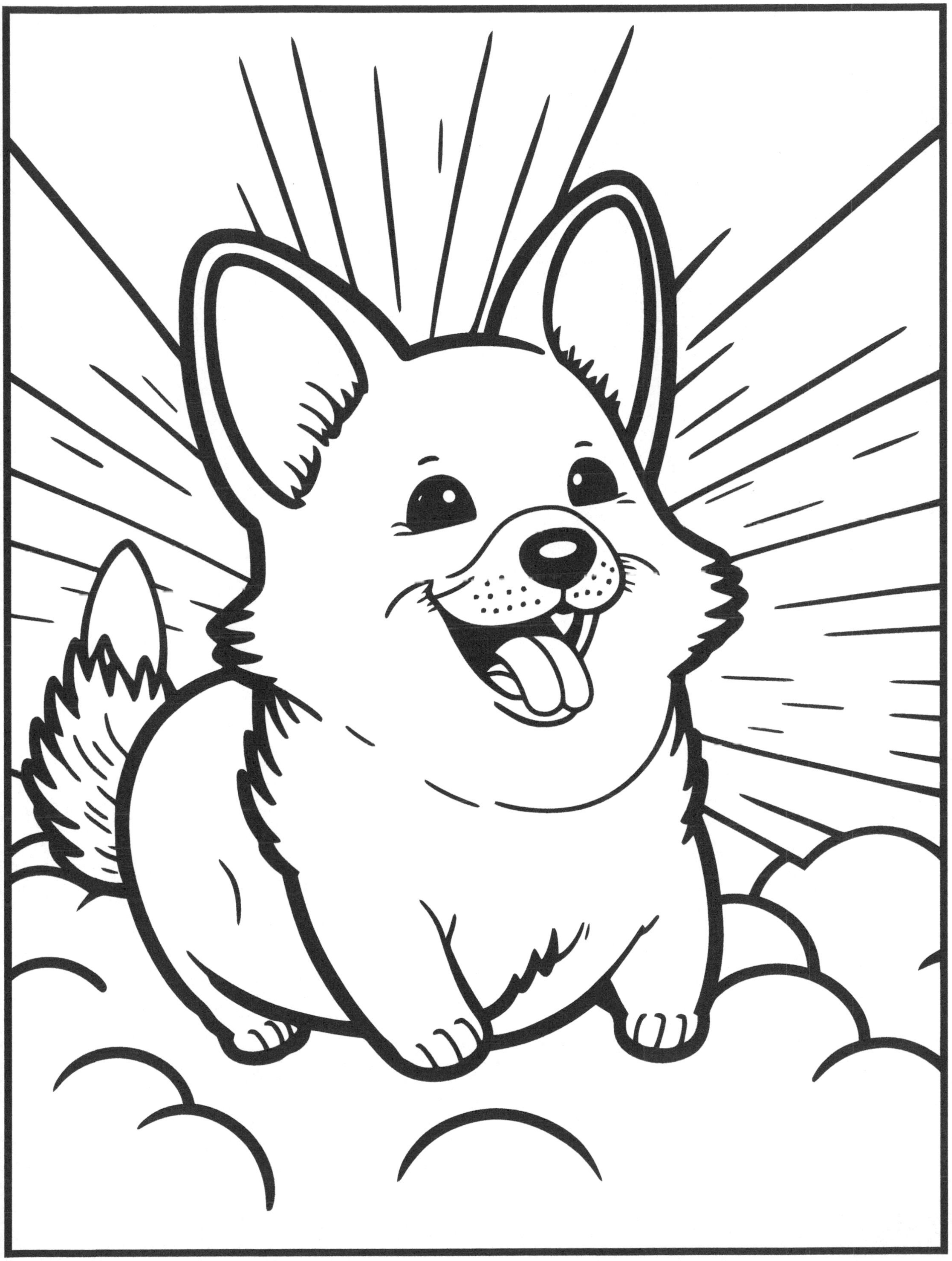

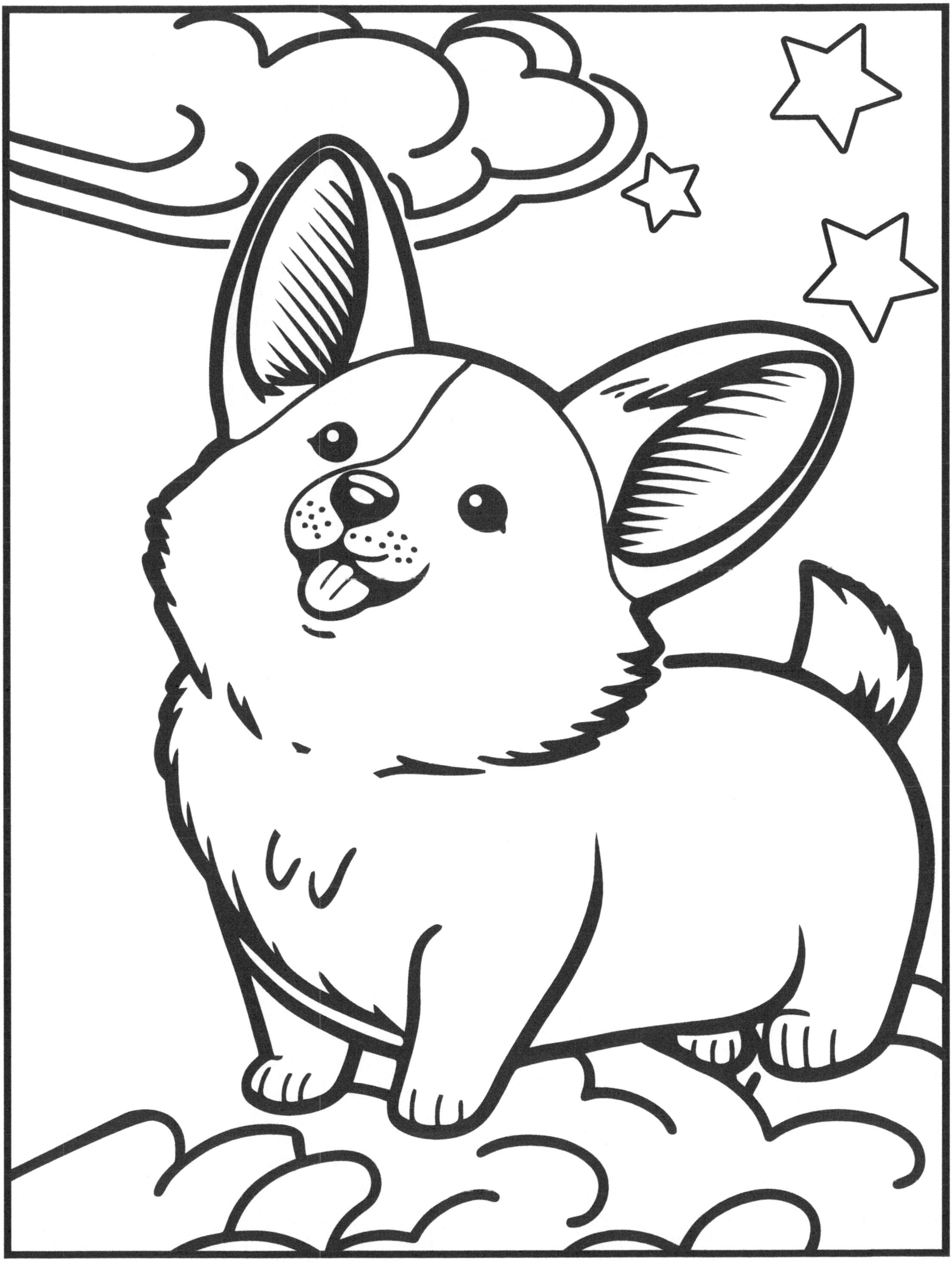

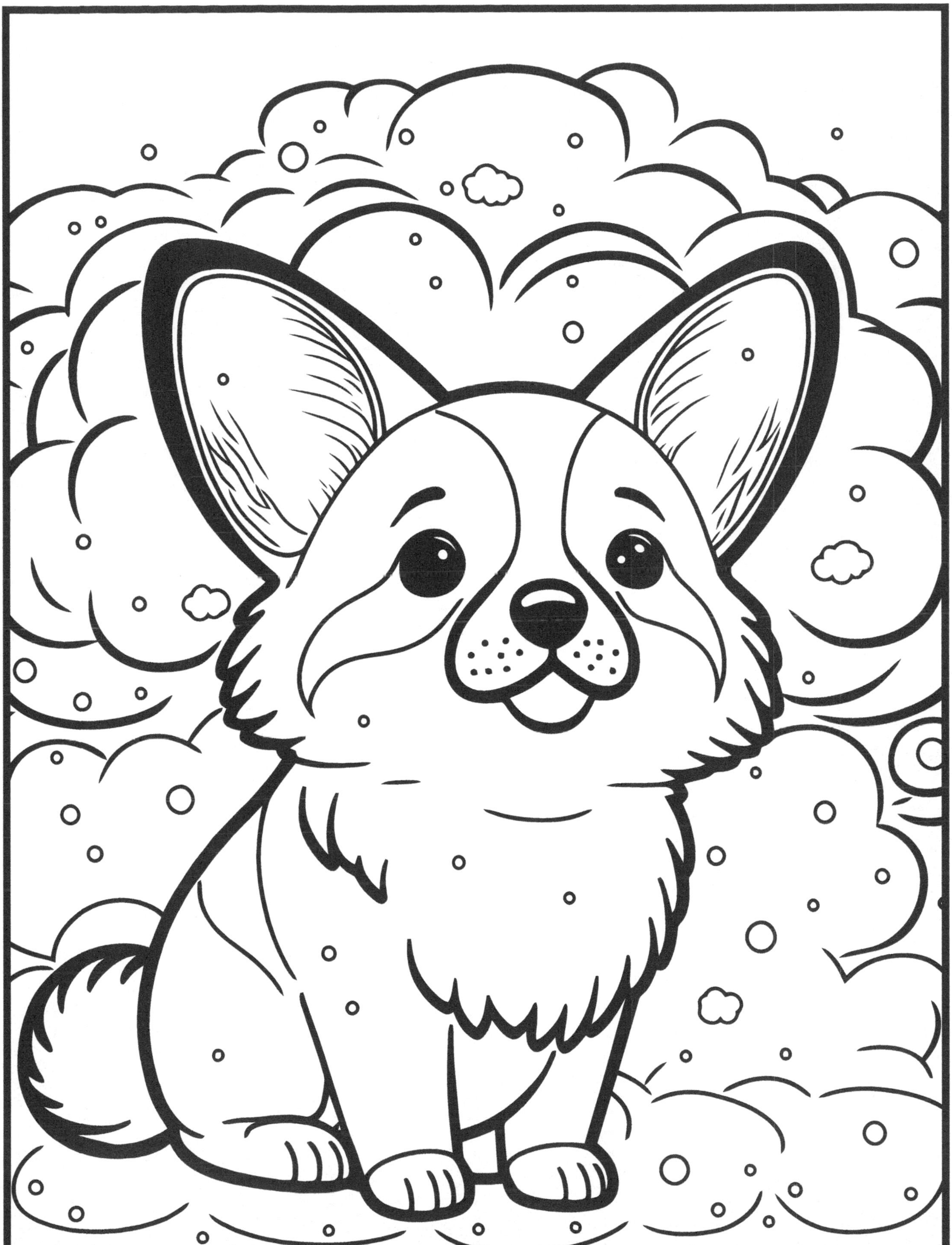

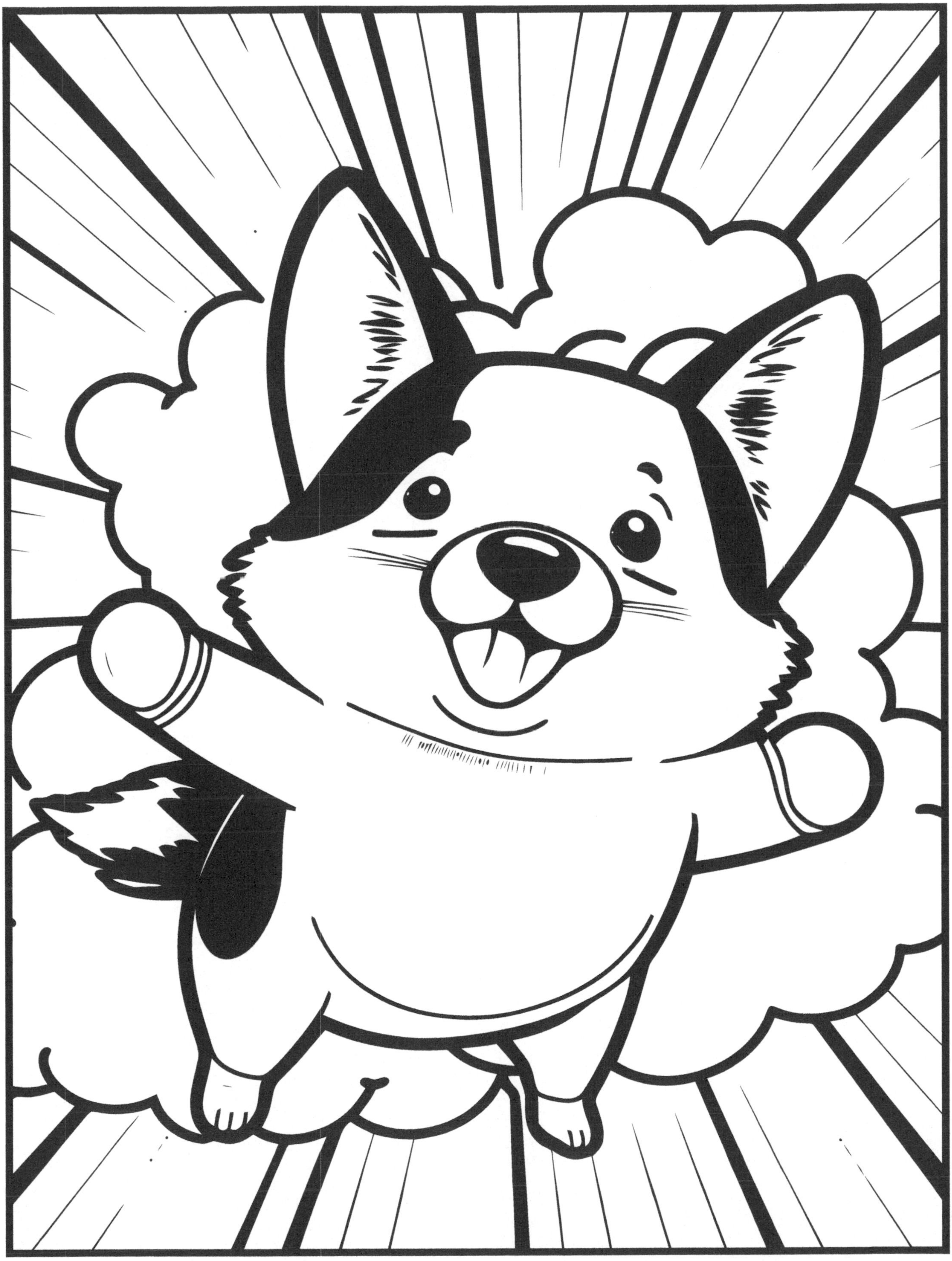

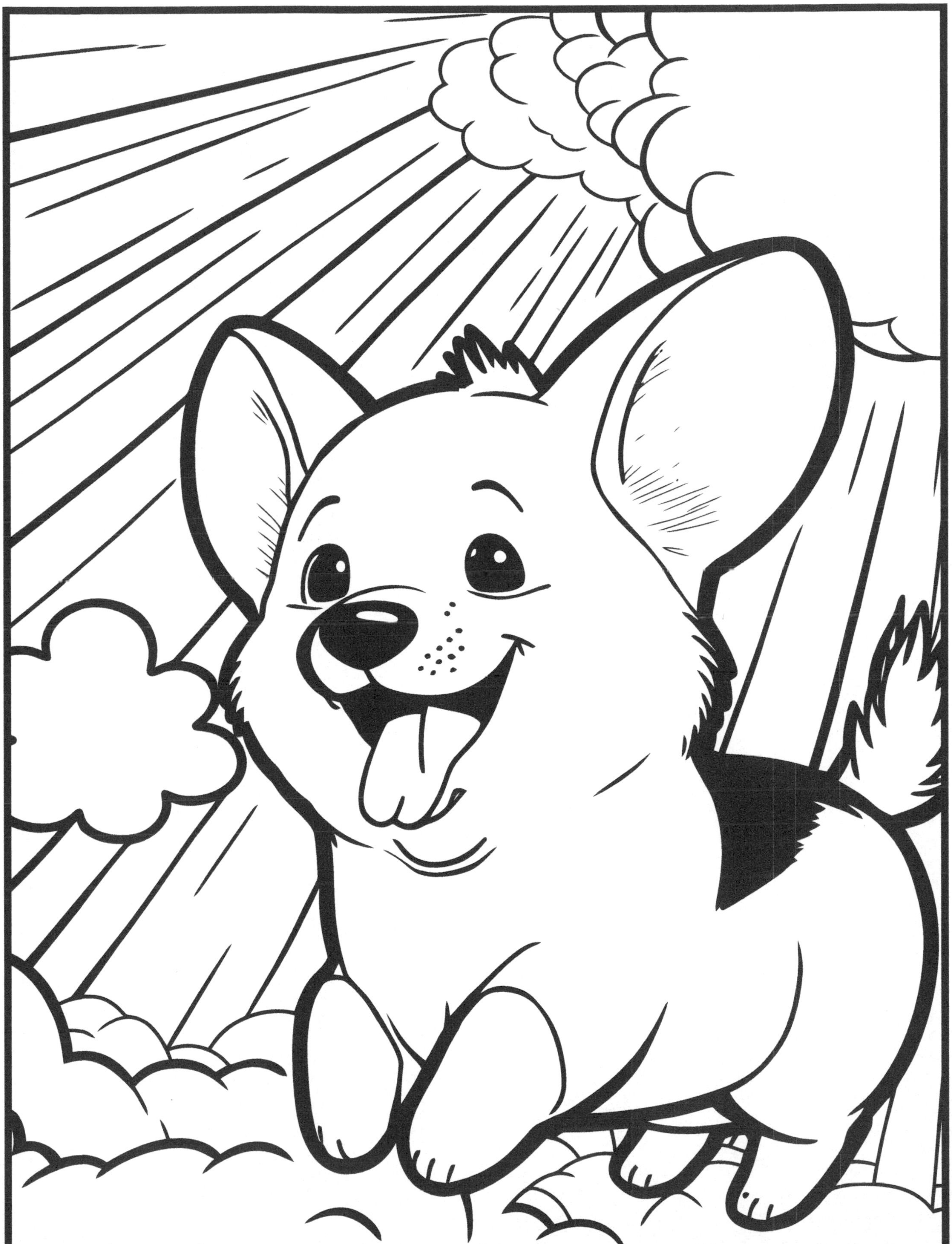

Made in the USA
Las Vegas, NV
15 April 2023

70629233R00050